Theatrical Costume and
the Amateur Stage

MICHAEL GEEN

Theatrical Costume and the Amateur Stage

A book of simple method in the making and altering of theatrical costumes, including a brief guide to costumes through the periods to the present day

Drawings by William Langstaffe

Publishers PLAYS, INC. *Boston*

First American edition published by
Plays, Inc., 1968
Reprinted 1972
Copyright © Isabel Geen 1968

Library of Congress Card Number: 68-31252
ISBN: 0-8238-0095-4

Printed in Great Britain

Introduction

This book is the result of many years of experience in the cutting, making and alteration of theatrical costumes.

The author was aware of the need among amateur and repertory companies throughout the country for a handbook such as this. The book's intention, however, is not to teach scientific paper pattern cutting as this cannot be learnt from books but only from practical work on a cutting table under the supervision of a qualified teacher. There are schools which are able to provide this instruction in both day and evening classes and there are also private schools of instruction although these may prove to be more expensive than schools run by local authorities. Nevertheless, *experienced* cutters may find books on the craft of cutting useful as a means of keeping abreast with up-to-date methods and with modern fashions.

There is another method of cutting done on a dressmakers dummy which is technically known as 'stand cutting'. This is also taught in the classroom but can be mastered by a clever or gifted dressmaker by the simple method of trial and error until one is satisfied with the result.

The book does not cover the making of men's costumes as these need a very experienced tailor or tailoress to work on them, especially period clothes, which will need to be hired or borrowed. Medieval costumes such as Roman, Greek, thirteenth century, fourteenth and fifteenth centuries through to the Elizabethan can be made in the manner of women's clothes but a man's tailors dummy will be needed to work on.

Contents

Theatrical Costume and
the Amateur Stage

Articles Necessary to Work With

A large cutting table, or flat surface, to cut and work on. A treadle sewing machine with a motor if it can be arranged, as a hand machine is too awkward, unless it too has a motor. A few shelves or a chest of drawers to keep oddments in, such as sewing silks, tacking cottons, hooks and eyes, hooks and bars, clip fasteners, etc. These are obtainable in black and steel metal, and in several sizes.

A dressmaker's dummy which will in future be referred to by its technical name 'A Stand'. In professional workrooms there are all the available sizes, but you can manage with one to commence with. It should be size 14 which means—bust 36, waist 26, hips, 38. This is a stock size which if needed to be made larger can be padded. If the garment being made is smaller than the stand, just fix the shoulders and leave the side seams to be adjusted to the required measurements on the cutting table.

Padding. Strips of material (scrap pieces) of 4 to 5 inches in width wound mummy fashion around the stand, until the required measurement is obtained.

A padded sleeve dummy for fixing sleeves. This cannot be bought but it is easy enough to make. Cut a calico sleeve pattern, sew it up, then cut a small oval shaped piece to fit the size of the opening at the wrist and machine it into the space. Stuff the sleeve with wadding flaked into shreds (not used as it is bought in one piece by the yard) until the sleeve dummy is very solid. Then cut another oval piece to fit the space at the armhole, and seam it with an inch seam shewing on the right side. This gives a margin when pinned on to the stand.

A tracing wheel. This is a metal wheel with spikes fixed to a handle which perforates when marking and tracing. Used on paper patterns, calico patterns, cotton materials, cheap taffetas or rayon linings, but never on silk.

A tape measure. Get a couple. One can never be found when needed. It is a sensible thing to keep a tape measure round your

11

neck when working, then you will know where it is when required.

Tailors chalk in white, blue and red. There is also black. Don't buy it, as it is liable to get messy and tends to get on to materials when it is left lying around. Always keep a sharp edge on the chalk as it is liable to wear down, and this can be done with a penknife or an old ever-ready razor blade.

A thimble in your size. Never sew without one, even if it is difficult getting used to wearing one. You will be glad when you have mastered it, otherwise your fingers will get very sore.

Needles. Six sharps for tacking, finer ones for sewing. You will eventually find the sizes preferred.

Pins. In boxes. Always see that they are steel. Others are inclined to rust and spoil material.

Cutting scissors. Several pairs if possible. Never cut string or paper with those kept for cutting materials. The edge soon goes and nothing is worse than blunt scissors. It is also expensive to keep them sharpened.

Wadding. This is not cotton wool (which is bought at a chemist and is quite expensive) but a cheaper variety sold by the yard, in black, off white and pure white.

Unbleached calico. Sold in three qualities—fine, coarse and very stiff, and in three widths, 36, 54 and 72. It is not white but cream or natural colour. Never use pure white as this gets very grubby in the making. The natural colour doesn't seem to.

A yardstick for marking up after cutting. Never attempt to mark a straight or diagonal line on any part of a garment other than by using a yardstick. Curved lines, of course, are done freehand.

A half-yardstick, or a stout clearly marked foot rule is required. This is for marking hem-lines as the yardstick is too awkward for this purpose and may give an uneven line. The rule will only be good for long dresses and any length up to twelve inches off the ground. The half-yardstick measures up to eighteen inches off the ground. There are few dresses shorter than this. Revue and ice-skating hem-lines are shorter, also some medieval tunics for men, when it is necessary for the yardstick to be used in order to get a straight hem-line. There are some patent hem markers on sale, but unless you have one already, it is an unnecessary item. I have tried one but soon went back to the old fashioned method of using the half-yardstick which I found more convenient.

A heavy electric iron, an ironing board and a sleeve board. An oval pad on which to press curved bust seams and darts. A velevet board which is 10″ wide by 24″ long in which wire is fixed (similar to a wire brush) and when pressing velvet on this board (wrong side towards the iron) there are no undue markings. There is also a small board for sleeves.

Two pieces of clean white cotton material, one for damping when pressing woollen material, the other for use when pressing dry. Do not press on to any material direct, even if it is on the wrong side. Always use either the damp or the dry cloth. See that there is no dressing in these pressing cloths or the iron or material will suffer. The best cloth for pressing is fine poplin as there is no dressing in this material. Dressing is a fine sort of powder used to give the material finish, and comes away on the iron.

Tacking cotton. A fine white cotton on reels or spools. Coloured cottons are useful for correcting after fittings.

Sewing silks. Use pure silk when possible, but Dewhurst's Sylko is very good, strong, and there is a good selection of colours on the small reels. There are also several colours in one ounce reels.

All the aforementioned articles can be purchased in the haberdashery department of all the large stores. It is also possible to obtain unbleached calico from furnishing departments. The fine calico is best for patterns as it moulds well, and it is also good for mounting, which is a method of cutting the calico first and placing under the original material. This way of making is also used for period clothes, as it gives them a good shape, and strengthens the garments for long use. The stronger calicos are good for petticoats and lining skirts, also for hooped underskirts. These calicos dye very well and they have been used for the actual clothes.

Calico is not used for mounting modern dresses, but if desired, a very fine poplin, lawn or silk organza (not nylon organza which shrivels under a hot iron) can be placed under wild silks and paper taffetas.

Poplin is very good even under fine wool, and especially in jackets.

Always cut in the mounting material first, then tack on to the outside material and press gently on the wrong side in case any tacking has to be undone because the materials are not lying flat.

Glossary of Words and their Meanings Used in Costume Workrooms

Allow—to leave seams and turnings.

Applique—to embroider with whipping or button-hole stitch, one material upon another in various designs, then cutting away surplus material around the design.

Baste—the tailor's term for tacking.

Bag—to machine two pieces of material together then turn out to the right side.

Bodkin—used for inserting elastic, etc., through slots.

Block—a head-shape used for millinery.

Basque—a flounce from the waist.

Bouffant—a puffed-out appearance.

Beading—the sewing on of beads or sequins in designs.

Bias—on the cross.

Backstitch—placing the needle immediately behind the former stitch.

Buttonhole—applies to buttonhole stitch or a piped buttonhole in material.

Bar-tack—to secure the end of a slit.

Bind—to sew a crossway piece on right side then hem back on to wrong.

Balance—marks which must be placed together when tacking.

Channel seam—two parts of the garment placed together with a piece underneath, and machined $\frac{1}{2}''$ apart.

Drawn thread—threads pulled from material and the space sewn on each side to secure.

Double-stitch—finishing a hem by machine—stitching once, cutting to the stitching, then stitching again.

Eyelet hole—a small hole, buttonholed all round.

Edge stitch—a tiny backstitch round the edge of lapels.

Finish—to oversew all seams, etc., leaving the garment tidy inside.

Flat tack—to mark for first fitting.

Fell—to sew a lining in a coat.

False hem—to add a piece to the hem to lengthen.

Fly front—a hidden buttonhole fastening.

Fringe—to unravel the edge.

Frill—to gather a narrow piece of material.

Face—to line an edge.

Flounce—as frill but wider.

Grain—when cutting, a thread is pulled so as not to get a twist in the material.

Gather—to run stitch and pull up for fullness.

Gauging—rows of gathering in sections.

Hand-roll—to turn in a fine edge.

Herringbone—a cross stitch.

Hemstitch—two edges tacked on to paper, leaving a small space, and feathered stitched together. Can also be done by machine.

Hem—the turning up at the bottom of garments.

Jewels—semi-precious stones of all sizes with holes, used for decorating.

Lining—to put material inside garments.

Markstitch—marking for first fitting with needle and cotton.

Marking-up—the term used for getting the first fitting ready, and for correcting afterwards.

Nip—to make an incision for easier pressing, in seams, on the wrong side.

Oversew—a stitch from left to right to prevent seams from fraying.

Pleat—material which is folded to form fulness.

Pad—a stitch used for sewing canvas to revers before the facing is put on.

Peplum—as basque.

Picot edge—this is formed when cutting through rows of machine hemstitching.

Placket—side opening, on skirts and dresses.

Pinking—a form of finishing edges of seams by cutting small points. There are scissors specially for this purpose.

Pipe—as bind, but with the turning away from the edge.

Raised seam—after seaming on wrong side, turn garment on

16

right side, keeping both seams together, and stitch along the edge.

Rouleau—a very fine bind, usually done on delicate work.

Slip stitch—a large running stitch.

Stitch back—a way of finishing seams by stitching back the edge.

Sprats head—a triangular design, done in twist to finish the tops of pleats.

Stub stitch—where the needle is pushed through to the wrong side, then from the wrong side to the right in single stitches.

Slash—a slit or hole faced out in another piece of self material.

Scollop—a semi-circular finish around an edge.

Shirr—this is done by using shirring elastic in the bobbin case of the machine, and silko on top.

Seams—the edges which are stitched together on the wrong side.

Turning—as seams.

Tack—to sew seams ready for fitting with white cotton.

Trace—after fitting to correct one side to the other.

Thong—making holes in the edges of leather, then oversewing with fine strips of leather.

Tuck—fine machining on double edges.

Vandyck—as scolloping but pointed edges.

Whipping—very close oversewing—one stitch next to the other.

Waistband—a petersham or double band of material finishing the waist of a skirt.

Yoke—the separate piece of material at top of jacket or dress near the shoulder. Or a waist-yoke, being a separate piece of material from waist to hip on a skirt.

Zip—the modern way of fastening clothes. Not used prior to the thirties.

17

Measurement Chart

All measurements in this book are in inches unless otherwise stated.

Using the tape measure firstly—from nape of neck at back to waist-line. Then from waist-line to hem-line as required.

Front—shoulder line to top of bust.

Then down to waist-line. Skirt as back.

Round the bust making sure tape measure is well over the shoulder blades at the back and over the top of bust in the front.

Round the waist-line (not too tightly).

Hips—two measurements—High hip (5″ down from the waist) Low hip—largest part.

Shoulder. From nape of neck to where sleeve is set in.

Across back—from where right sleeve is set in across to where the left sleeve is set in.

Outside sleeve—from where sleeve is set in down to the wrist (with arm bent) taking tape measure round the elbow.

Inside sleeve—from where sleeve is set in to the wrist—arm outstretched.

Round the arm—as high as possible. Round the elbow with arm bent, and round the wrist.

If measurements are for a singer take a diaphragm measurement, i.e. under bust, right round about 4″ above the waist, and not too tightly.

There are other ways of taking measurements but these are the simple methods. At each point mentioned place the tape measure and write the amount in inches on a piece of paper, or a book kept for this purpose.

EXAMPLE OF AN AVERAGE MEASUREMENT CHART
(Women)

Back neck to waist	..	..	..	..	16
Waist to hem. Short dresses ..	..	..	..	27
Floor length ..	..	..	..	40

Front shoulder to top of bust..		..	..	..			12
Front shoulder to front waist			..	..	..		17½
Round bust	..	..	..	..	..	..	36
Round waist	..	..	..	..	..	..	26
Round high hip		..	..	..	..	..	37½
Round low hip ..		..	..	..	..	..	39
Shoulder ..	..	..	..	..	..	..	4¾
Across back	..	..	..	..	..	..	15½
Outside sleeve	..	..	..	..	..	..	24
Inside sleeve	..	..	..	..	..	..	19
Round top of arm		..	..	..	..	..	15
Elbow	..	..	..	..	..	..	11½
Wrist	..	..	..	..	..	..	7
A singer–diaphragm		..	..	..	..	..	33
Head	..	..	..	..	..	..	22
Shoes	..	..	..	..	..	..	5
Neck	..	..	..	..	..	..	13

MEASUREMENT CHART (Men)

Example of average figure.

Chest	40
Waist	32
Breech (Hips)	38
From centre back, across shoulder blade. (Half back).. ..	8
To elbow	21
To wrist	32
Jacket length.	
Back of neck to waist ..	18
„ „ to hem ..	27
„ „ to front waist..	23
Inside sleeve	19
Trousers.	
Outside leg	43
Inside leg	32
Thigh	24
Knee	18
Bottom	16

19

Inside leg.
Outside leg.
Waist.
Breech.
Thigh.
Calf.
Ankle, and foot length.
Chest—Girth—shoulder, under crotch
and back to the shoulder.
Centre back to armhole seam, con-
tinuing to elbow and wrist.
Round forearm, round elbow, and
round wrist.

No measurements given for these as they are individual.

Cutting and Marking Up

Place the pattern of whatever part of the garment is being cut, on to the material, or calico, if this is being cut first. Always work with the centre back towards you, and the selvedge of the material towards you, which means the open side. The centre back of all theatrical costumes is best left open down to the hips. This is a practical way of dressing for artists—they just step in— and even if some of the clothes do have to go over the head, there is plenty of space so as not to get make-up on the clothes and the hair styles do not get spoilt.

The front of the garment is usually cut with the folded side of the material towards you at the centre front, unless seams are being made down the front. Some styles may require this, depending on the sketch being adapted. If there is any doubt as to the success of the result of any sketch being made, a good thing is to cut it out in calico first. This is done in professional workrooms. The finished pattern, or 'try-out' is technically called a 'toile'— a French word pronounced to rhyme with 'snarl'. Sometimes only one side of the toile is made (the right side) from centre back to centre front, and the right sleeve. This gives an idea of the sketch, also saves spoiling the material. If not a success first time it will lead the way to be improved upon.

Always see that the materials are on the double with the right side facing inwards. When cutting from the block pattern, after marking round the measured size, always leave plenty of margin before cutting out. $1\frac{1}{2}''$ to 2″ under-arm seams, $1\frac{1}{2}''$ to 2″ shoulder and armholes, $1\frac{1}{2}''$ to 2″ at waist, $1\frac{1}{2}''$ to 2″ side seams and any other seams in the skirt, 4″ at the hem, $1\frac{1}{2}''$ to 2″ under-arm seams at sleeves and definitely 2″ or more at the bottom of sleeves which after being turned up to required length is left. Sleeves have a habit of working up during fittings and this leaves a margin to lengthen the sleeves if necessary. Also leave 1″ at the head or top of sleeve. These margins are always best left, when the costume is finished as they allow for altering for a larger person. Don't cut away seams or darts at any time. You will regret it at some future date.

Never in any circumstances mark with chalk or pencil on the right side of the material.

You will find that woollen materials and some cottons are 54" wide and the pattern can be laid over this space quite easily. Silks and cottons are mostly 36" wide, in which case fold the material to the width of the pattern being cut, making a new fold for the centre front, which is cut first this time. You will find you will get one half of the back on the piece over the width. Then place this piece on another piece similar—right sides inside— with both edges facing you, then cut the back.

The sleeves are also cut double in the same way.

Never under buy the yardage of material, which is a mistake. An extra piece may be needed later on. Sometimes accidents happen, or the fit is not good and it will be regretted not buying sufficient.

When the garment is cut out make a roll or package of the pieces over, so that they are all together. Tie round, store in a nearby place easily accessible or found when required. Never throw away such pieces while the garment is still in stock, as pieces may be wanted for repairs. They may also be useful for trimming other costumes.

Marking Up

There are several ways of doing this. One side of the material may have already been marked from the pattern. Correct all straight and diagonal lines with the yardstick. Go over curved lines to see that they are a good shape. In order to trace these marks on the other side of the garment the following methods are used.

The professional and correct way is 'mark-stitching' which is done with needle and tacking cotton. This is a highly skilled method needing personal explanation, it takes time to do, and when finished there are tiny ends of cotton to be removed from the material which needs patience.

A good way is to pin all the marks—about 2″ apart—following the line downwards (not across), turning the garment over. Then make a dot with chalk or pencil in all the pin marks. Remove all pins and correct the dots with the yard-stick and freehand on the curves.

A very good way of marking up for amateurs would be as follows:— Thread a needle with double tacking cotton—not more than 8″ in length. Leave ends free with no knots. Take a piece of old white chalk (blue or red if working on calico). Don't use a piece of new chalk. Keep a box of broken chalk for this purpose. Rub the cotton along the chalk several times and sew in the marks to be traced through. Do this every three or four stitches, always towards the way you are working, down from waist to hem on the skirt, shoulder to waist on the bodice, and head to wrist on the sleeve. This marking should be done 1″ or 1½″ apart right through to the other side. There will be a series of dots where you have been working. Always see that the needle is drawn out towards the hem, never across or backwards, or you will tear the material you are working on. Use this method on all marking out lines and curves, and when the material is taken apart, there will be clear dots on the right and wrong sides.

Always put a neat X in chalk on the wrong sides of all pieces of material, as a guide to prevent the garment from being made up wrongly. The pieces must always be 'paired', which means matching left and right sides of garment, and sleeves.

This marking up process can be done on woollens, cottons, unbleached calico, under-petticoats and patterns, but definitely never on silks or rayons which need a more delicate marking up process.

A good method on silks and rayons is to pin as before-mentioned, placing a finger through the two sides of the material, tacking wherever the pin line is indicated on the single material. Then turn the piece over and do likewise on the other side, not removing the pins until both sides have been marked. This is a slow laborious way, but if the material is delicate, it is necessary to work in this way.

Fitting and Correcting

When the costume, or calico under-lining is tacked up ready for fitting, place it on the artist concerned, fit right side only and the right sleeve, mark armhole and neck-line required, check waist-line, under bust line, shoulder and side seam. Then the hem-line which is always marked last.

If the garment is being made from measurements only, pad the stand to the required size and fit the stand instead of a person, and use the sleeve dummy,

All fitting is done with pins.

After fitting remove the costume from the dummy, or person, and to correct put pencil or chalk dots wherever there are pins, on the wrong side. When all the pins are marked, remove them, and take the costume apart. Lay flat, on the double, as originally cut, and mark all the corrections, so that both sides are the same. If the garment is to be fitted again, retack and fit. If it is to be finished, machine, and press seams of each piece as the work proceeds. In order to save trouble, it is advisable to give two fittings.

Bodice Pattern

Cut two pieces of unbleached calico measuring 24″ in length by 18″ across. Place one piece at centre back of the stand, long side downwards as far up as the top of the neck of the stand, pinning it there, then pin the bottom of the piece of calico to the stand. Also pin at 4″ intervals down centre back edge. Also pin at the shoulder, neck and armhole. Mark a pencil line on the neck seam and shoulder seam, which is clearly marked on the stand and round the armhole line at the edge of the stand. Then from the centre back of waist, across the waist, but pinning a dart (which is a seam of $\frac{1}{2}$″ upwards from waist to nothing) about 4″ high. This is done at 4″ from centre back. You can then follow the side seam on the stand from neck to waist. When you have done this remove calico from the stand and mark all lines clearly with the yardstick—armholes freehand—and cut right in the pencil line. This is called a nett block pattern, and is always cut without seam allowance. The front is done in exactly the same way— from centre front—round neck-line to shoulder and armhole, darting under bust to shape of stand—exactly as back—at the waist and side seams. Then remove from stand and proceed exactly as for back.

When using the block pattern mark round the edges on to the material being used, but this time, leaving the seam allowances. Also do this when using the block sleeve pattern and block skirt pattern which appear on the following pages. To transfer the block pattern from calico on to brown paper, just follow the edges. As I have said earlier paper patterns are easier for hanging up.

Skirt Pattern

Cut two pieces of calico 36" long by 14" across. Pin at centre back and front of waist on the stand—as bodice—but downwards this time, with pins at 4" intervals. Make a dart at waist, back and front, similar to those in the bodice, $\frac{1}{2}$" at the waist down to nothing at 4". Follow side seams of stand and mark required hem-line. Remove pieces from stand and cut nett. Always match darts with those on the bodice so that when sewn up they run in one straight line.

Block Sleeve Pattern

Take a piece of brown paper 27″ by 18″. Draw a line in pencil down the centre, then at 24″ apart (length of sleeve) draw two more lines across the centre line. At 5″ from the top line, draw another line across. On this line make a mark at 14″ across, i.e. 7″ each side from centre line. At the bottom line mark 10″ across, i.e. 5″ each side from the centre line. From each mark at the top to each mark at the bottom draw a diagonal line (both sides). These are the under-arm seams. From the highest point at the top of the centre line to the top of the under-arm seam, draw a diagonal line, on each side. Divide these lines into three equal parts. At the division nearest the centre put a mark 1″ higher than the line on both sides. Then make a free-hand curved line from centre point over to the division mark nearer the seam of the sleeve. This will give the sleeve head.

At the bottom line mark the centre of each half, then mark $\frac{1}{2}$″ down at one side and $\frac{1}{2}$″ up at the other side. Draw a free-hand curved line here, the higher mark being the front of the sleeve. To make the sleeve narrower make a dart at back, from elbow to wrist, fitting the arm. This gives room for bending the arm.

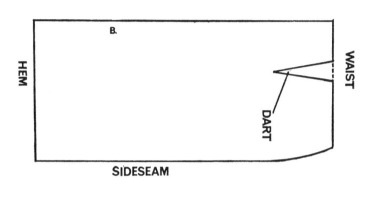

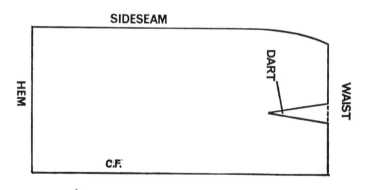

Fig. 1. Block skirt pattern.

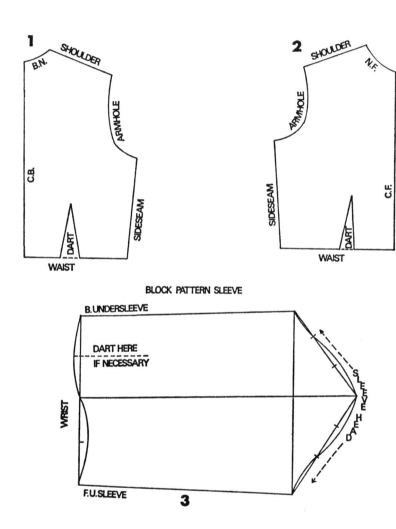

Fig. 2. Block bodice (1 and 2) and sleeve (3) pattern

Names of Materials Used in Making Up of Period and Modern Clothes

Afgalaine—Woollen material with a clear weave in various colours. 54" wide.

American Cloth—Stiff leathery material in all colours, shiny or matt surface. Also in gold and silver. 27" wide.

Alpaca—A wiry textured material of alpaca goats wool and cotton used for overalls, housekeepers' dresses and industrial jackets. 54" wide. In dark shades only. Looks best in black.

Angora—A woollen material 54" wide with a fleecy surface owing to the wool from angora goats being woven into it. Also obtainable as hanks of knitting wool.

Bedford Cord—Woollen material with a vertical cord used for men's trousers and riding breeches. Cheaper variety in cotton for farm and agricultural workers' breeches, in fawn. 54" wide.

Barathea—A worsted material in a fine check weave, in khaki, used for military uniforms, and in black for men's evening wear. 60" wide.

Batiste—A very fine cotton muslin with a crisp silky finish. 36"

Bayadere—A dull silk material alternating $\frac{1}{4}$" satin stripes with $\frac{1}{4}$" self stripes. 36" wide, most colours.

Bolton Sheeting—Very firm cotton material with diagonal weave, in various colours. 48" wide.

Bouclé—A woollen material with a pebbly surface which is reversable and made in several colours. 54" wide.

Brocade—Fancy woven or embossed material, in a variety of designs and colours, some interwoven with gold, silver and lurex thread. In three widths—36", 42" and 54" wide.

Buckram—Very stiff canvas in white and tan used for millinery and costumes which need substantial backing.

Cambric—A white cotton in various qualities and widths. Useful for mounting, pattern making and lining. 36" wide.

Calico—A white stiff cotton similar to cambric. 36" wide.

Calico (Unbleached)—In natural colour, three qualities and three widths—36", 54" and 72". Used for pattern making.

Cheesecloth—Thin cotton with a gauze finish. 36" wide in white only. Dyes well.

Crepe de Chine—Pure Chinese silk in many colours suitable for underclothes. Obtainable in floral and spotted designs. 36" wide.

Chiffon—Fine silk transparent material which floats. 40" wide. Many colours. It is necessary for a lot of material to be used to get a good result. Obtainable in floral designs.

Canvas—A buff colour material of cotton and flax in various textures, some with horsehair interwoven. Used for tailoring and mounting. 30" and 36" wide.

Corduroy—Velveteen with a vertical corded finish. Corded in various widths, from needlecord $\frac{1}{16}"$ to hollow-cut at $\frac{1}{2}"$. Three widths—22" 27" and 36". Must be cut with pile upwards. Most colours.

Chintz—Cotton material in floral designs. Obtainable with a glazed finish. 36" and 48" wide. Bought in soft-furnishing departments.

Crepe—A name used for several materials. Moss crepe, material with a mossy finish, reversible. Also known as 'peau de peche'. Satin backed crepe, a rough surfaced material with a satin back. Crepe romaine, a sheer material. All these are 36" wide. Wool crepe with a rough pebbly finish in various colours, 54" wide.

Cavalry Twill—A very strong worsted material used for men's suits and overcoats, mostly in fawn colour. Obtainable in black and tan. 60" wide.

Covert Coating—Worsted material used for Edwardian period coats and suits, and ladies' costumes and dresses—in grey, brown and fawn. 60" wide.

Caracule—Imitation astrachan fur cloth with a small curl, in black, grey, brown and cream. 54" wide.

Cotton Voile—Transparent cotton, good for veiling, a variety of colours. Also in floral designs. 36" wide.

Cashmere—A very fine and expensive material made from the wool of tibetan goats, used for men's jackets and overcoats.

60" wide. Also obtainable in hanks of knitting wool. Not hard wearing as the surface is inclined to rub with wear.

Damask—A cotton brocade in various colours with a floral design, woven in self colour. 48" wide. Obtainable in soft-furnishing departments.

Domette—Fleecy cotton inter-lining in white. 36" wide.

Delaine—Soft woollen material in a variety of designs. Both floral and Paisley. 36" and 54". The word 'Laine' which is used at the end of the name of several materials is derived from a French word for woollen cloth—'Lainage'.

Foulard—Floral silk used in the Edwardian period and twenties for dresses and dressing gowns. At present almost unobtainable.

Facecloth—Heavy woollen material with a shiny surface, in a variety of colours. Must be cut with the face downwards, as otherwise it would wear woolly. There are some fine light-weights, almost like silk in texture. 54" wide.

Faille—Pronounced 'Fie'. A firm pure silk material, with a matt finish. Reversible. 42" and 36" wide. Known also as 'Peau de soie' (Skin of silk). There is a cheaper quality made in rayon in a variety of colours.

Faconne—Velvet flowers embossed on to silk or satin. In numerous colours. 36" wide.

Fur Fabric—Imitation fur materials, giving a luxury look to coats and costumes, when used for lining. Suitable for trimming. In white, black and grey, and with leopard, ocelot and other animal markings. 54" wide. Made also in nylon and rayon.

Flannel—Off-white fleecy material of wool, and in red for old ladies' petticoats, grey for inexpensive trousers. 54" wide.

Flannel (Worsted)—A superior material to the plain flannel, in sombre shades of brown, navy and grey. Also obtainable with white chalk stripes. In various weights and qualities. Suitable for men's suits and blazers. The lighter weights can be used for ladies' modern and period costumes. 54" wide.

Georgette—In pure silk similar to chiffon but with a firmer finish. Difficult to obtain nowadays. 36" wide.

33

Georgette (Cotton, Rayon, Nylon)—In plain colours and floral designs. 36″ wide.

Georgette (Wool)—A sheer material used mainly in the twenties and thirties. In a variety of colours. 54″ wide.

Gaberdine—A woollen material with a diagonal weave (patented by Burberrys) in various colours, suitable for men's suits and light overcoats, and used for ladies' costumes. 54″ wide.

Gaberdine—By a modern method of weaving elastic into the yarn this material is now used for ski pants and dancers' stretch trousers. 54″ wide.

Gingham—A cotton made in various sized checks and colours, very popular for shirts, blouses and summer dresses. Both modern and period. 36″ wide.

Hopsack—A clear cross weave woollen material in various colours. Suitable for blazers and suits. 54″ wide.

Hessian—A coarse sacking useful for rough clothes, and sometimes used for scenery. 36″ and 48″ wide.

Italian Cloth—A heavy cotton sateen used by tailors for linings, in sombre colours, brown, black, navy, grey and fawn. 54″ wide.

Ice Wool—An interlining of feather weight fleecy wool. Looks like gauzy knitting. In black and white. 54″ wide.

Jersey—A woollen material resembling fine knitting, in various colours, and made in a Swiss double knit. Suitable for jackets, suits and coats. 54″ wide.

Jersey (Fine silk and rayon)—Both these drape well for Grecian style costumes. 48″ wide.

Jersey (Cotton)—In plain colours and with one inch wide horizontal stripes in blue and red on a white ground. Suitable for pirates' and sailors' jerseys. 48″ wide.

Lastex—An elastic yarn interwoven with satin material, excellent for leotards and bathing suits. 36″ and 42″ wide.

Lurex—A glittery thread interwoven into several materials to give a sparkling finish.

Lisse—An uncrushable chiffon (very strong) used for leotards and low decollete necklines (almost invisible). 36″ wide.

34

Lame—A material woven with gold or silver thread. Is called 'Cloth of Gold' or 'Cloth of Silver'. 36″ wide.

Lace—In cotton, rayon and wool. In various colours and widths, and qualities. 'Chantilly', Brussels, Nottingham. There is a very heavy expensive lace called 'Guipure'. Various edgings and insertions from ¼″ to 36″. This is only made in white, cream, and coffee colour.

Matelasse—Quilted material in floral and ripple designs. Silk or taffeta worked on to net. Also called 'Cloque'. 36″ wide.

Mohair—A material with a silky finish made from hair of Angora goats and wool, used for men's light-weight suits. 54″ wide and 60″.

Melton—Heavy woollen material used for livery and military overcoats. In dark colours only. 60″ wide.

Muslin—A sheer cotton in white and colours. Dyes well. 36″ wide.

Muslin (Book)—A stiff cotton fabric in black and white only, used for mounting and millinery. 36″ wide.

Mull—A soft muslin used for pattern making. In white only. 36″ wide.

Merino—This material is made from the wool of Spanish merino sheep. 54″ wide.

Moire—A firm material in silk or rayon in a variety of colours, with a watermark of irregular wavy lines in pattern. 36″ and 42″ wide.

Nylon—A modern yarn used in a quantity of materials, giving an uncrushable finish.

Nylon (Brushed)—Made in various floral and other designs, resembling wool. 36″ wide.

Noile—A coarse cotton in natural colour having a rough home-spun look. Makes up into period shirts, etc. Dyes well. 48″ wide. Obtainable in soft-furnishing departments.

Organdy—A stiff muslin used mainly for trimming. In white and a few colours. Some with woven spots and floral designs. 36″ wide.

Organza—Pure silk, or nylon transparent material. Sometimes has Lurex thread interwoven. 42″ wide.

35

Ottoman—A silky material with a flat horizontal cord about $\frac{1}{8}''$ wide, reversible. 36" wide. In a few colours.

Pique—(Pronounced 'Pee-kee'). A cotton corded material in several qualities. White only. Used for tennis dresses, shorts and trimmings. 36" wide.

Palm Beach—A suiting of light weight used for tropical wear, in very pale shades. 60" wide.

Poplin—A very useful cotton material in a variety of colours, used for shirts, blouses, petticoats. There is also a heavier quality which makes light-weight coats. 36" wide.

Plush—A hairy finish on cotton or silk used chiefly in millinery. 18" and 36" wide.

Repp—A material of silk or wool with a horizontal cord, also made in cotton. 36" and 48" wide.

Rayon—A yarn woven into artificial silk. There are several qualities. Used mainly for linings and underslips. In most colours, and floral designs. 36" wide.

Silk Net—(Also called 'Tulle'). A very fine transparent material in various widths used for bridal veils and millinery. Is also obtainable in cotton and rayon in many colours. Suitable for ballet dresses and fluffy evening dress skirts. Recently there has been a nylon flame-proof net made. 36" and 54" wide.

Shantung—Undyed China silk, excellent for tropical wear. 30" wide.

Sharkskin—A white cotton and artificial silk material with a ribbed finish, used for men's summer dinner jackets and ladies' tennis dresses, shorts and suits. 36" wide.

Satin—In pure silk in many colours and in a variety of floral designs. 36" wide.

Satin (Artificial silk)—Suitable for linings. In many colours. 36" wide.

Satin (Slipper and Duchess)—Heavy fabrics in pure silk and rayon, suitable for modern and period gowns and costumes. 36" and 42" wide.

Satin (Romaine)—A pure silk light-weight material in a variety of colours. 36" wide.

Satin (Cotton)—A heavy material with a cotton back suitable for

36

clowns and pierrots costumes. A very firm fabric with a glossy finish. In many colours. Obtainable in soft-furnishing departments and theatrical material suppliers. 36″ and 48″ wide.

Sateen—A cheaper variety of cotton satin. Very useful, but the shiny surface disappears if pressed damp. Many colours. 36″ wide.

Stockinette—An artificial material resembling knitting, used for draping and Grecian type dresses. In many colours. 48″ wide.

Serge—A woollen material in dark colours, suitable for chauffeur's suits and gym slips. 54″ wide.

Stayflex—A modern canvas and interlining which is prepared so as to stick to the cloth when a heated iron is pressed to the material. In white and cream, in various widths and textures.

Sparterie—A stiff straw-like material used by milliners to make foundation shapes. 30″ wide.

Tussore—Indian rough silk in various colours. Used for tropical wear. 30″ wide.

Tweed—Heavy wool in a variety of colours and weaves, checks, tartans and plaids. There are some finer worsted tweeds in small check designs. 54″ wide.

Tweed (Harris)—Homespun by village people. Also Scotch and Irish tweeds. All these are 27″ wide due to the size of the looms on which they are woven.

Tweed (Silk)—A coarse silk which is woven to represent tweed, used for light-weight men's and women's modern clothes. This material originally came from Italy. Not made in many colours. 54″ wide.

Tweed—There is a cheap form of tweed with a whiskery finish called 'Frieze' used for peasants and workmenlike costumes, in drab colours. 54″ wide.

Tarlatan—A stiff cotton muslin with a gauze finish in a variety of colours, good for children's ballet and fancy dresses. 54″ wide.

Tricel—A modern fabric with a silky appearance in a variety of floral and other designs. 36″ wide.

Terylene—Another modern yarn which when interwoven with wool or silk makes them crease resistant. 36″ and 54″ wide.

Terry Towelling—Made in various colours and widths and in floral and striped designs.

Turkish Towelling—A heavier quality than the former. Mostly in plain colours. 36″ and 48″ wide.

Taffeta—Pure silk, rayon, and a feather-weight quality called 'Paper Taffeta' the latter also being made in pure silk or rayon. Variety of colours and in floral and check designs. 36″ wide.

Taffeta (Shot)—Showing two colours as it is worn owing to the weave and colours of the yarns being different, horizontally and vertically (the warp and the woof). 36″ wide.

Taffeta (Poult)—A heavier quality with a corded finish in a variety of colours. Makes evening coats and period petticoats. 36″ and 42″ wide.

Tie-silk—An improved material similar to foulard in floral and other designs, in a variety of colours. Made in pure silk or rayon. There is a firmer material with a diagonal twill which is called 'Surah' silk, which is reversible. 36″ wide.

Thai Silk—A heavy rough corded dull silk from Thailand, in a variety of colours. 36″ wide. Mr. Oliver Messel, the celebrated designer, favours this material and uses it often. It can be purchased at Thailand Silks Co., 11 Beauchamp Place, London, S.W.1.

Velveteen—A cotton backed material in several widths and various qualities.

Velvet—There have been various types of this material worn throughout the years. Chiffon velvet (not now easily obtainable) very popular in Edwardian period for cloaks and dresses. Panne velvet, very rare nowadays, with a high glossy finish, mirrorlike in its effect. Ring velvet, worn in the twenties, so named because one yard of this material could go through a lady's ring. Woven on to a Chiffon base. Mantle velvet, a heavy material with a taffeta back, used for coats and cloaks. There are also brocaded velvets, figured velvets and striped velvets. Today there are some splendid improved qualities which are water repellant and crease resistant, woven with a straight pile, enabling them to be cut in any way. This material must otherwise be cut with the pile going upwards, which makes it look darker and richer. 36″ wide. There are furnishing velvets which are very heavy, woven on to a cotton back. Meant for drapes but can be used for costumes. In a variety of colours. 48″ wide.

Vicuna—A very soft material woven from llama wool. Used for men's jackets and overcoats. Similar, but harder wearing than cashmere. 60″ wide.

Velour—A heavy woollen material suitable for period coats and costumes. A cheaper quality is used for dressing gowns. A cotton velour referred to as 'Molleton' can also be obtained. All these materials can be had in a variety of colours. 54″ wide.

Vilene—A modern, stiff interlining in various textures. White, grey and black. Useful for stiffening skirts and jackets. Several widths.

Wadding—A form of cotton wool in black and white, used for padding, etc., where bulk is necessary. 18″ wide.

Wincyette—A cotton flannel with a woolly surface. Suitable for pyjamas and nightdresses. In plain colours and small printed designs. 36″ wide.

Wild Silk—Pure silk with a slub surface. Has a homespun appearance and is very light in weight. Made in a variety of colours. Used in modern dressmaking and it also looks excellent made up into period clothes. 36″ wide. In a recent production of 'School for Scandal' all the ladies' costumes were made in this light-weight material which appeared to float as the actresses walked across the stage. These clothes were highly praised by the critics in the U.S.A. and Miss Margaret Rutherford and the other ladies in the company found them a pleasure to wear.

Wild Silk—A type (similar to the pure silk) but in rayon. Both qualities obtainable in a good selection of colours. 36″ wide.

One of the chief theatrical material suppliers is:—
Messrs. B. Burnet,
22 Garrick Street,
London, W.C.2.

Another useful material which is stocked by Messrs. Burnet is *Felt*, in all colours. 54″ wide.

A Basic Dress

A princess, or chemise dress, which is all in one, cut from shoulder to hem, with no waist, straight side seams, from arm-hole to waist, then flaring slightly to hem to allow movement at legs. If cut straight all down it could be slit at sides about 12" from hem.

This garment should be cut with a wrap-over at back which is an addition from centre back of 5" on both sides at the back, which will allow the dress to be used for various sizes, using patent fasteners which are adjustable. Don't forget to leave large seams machined with a big stitch to enable easy unpicking.

If the waist is to be defined make darts $\frac{1}{2}$" deep, or to fit the measurements required, from waist upwards to the bust and from the waist downwards to the hips, about 8" apart at back and front. Do not cut these darts but use a large machine stitch as for side seams. Darts should not be taken in more than 1" at waist. If it is necessary to make the garment still tighter, take the rest out of the side seams, shaping upwards and downwards from the waist, like the darts, but not cutting any material away. Press these seams and darts on the oval pad which will give them the required shape, without cutting away the seam or darts. This surplus inlay may be wanted at some future time.

These basic dresses may be needed short, or floor length and the same method is used in both cases.

These basic dresses should be made sleeveless, with finished armholes and neck-line. The neck-line can be cut either to a 'V' line about 8" to shoulder to centre front, or to a high round neck no lower than 6" in front.

Three pairs of sleeves should be made with each dress. One pair long, tight to fit; one pair long, very wide at the wrist and dropping at back for medieval use, and one pair of short puffed sleeves (gathered top and bottom) for Empire or Regency use.

There are two more types of sleeves, if they are necessary, to be made. Three-quarter and short plain sleeves for modern wear.

All sleeves are made in pairs and finished (except for the head) on which loops are sewn, then put on a shoulder hanger, or hook, to keep them from creasing. Allow large seams in the sleeves, wherever possible, and machine with a big stitch.

The basic dress can be easily adjusted for the following periods:—

REGENCY. The long dress with contrasting narrow sash placed under the bust line, tied into a bow and ends at the back over the wrap-over. Use either the long sleeves or the short puff. Worn with a bonnet or shawl for the day, and a stole or cape for the evening.

THE TWENTIES. Short dress with wide sash tacked at a low hip-line—18" up from hem—with no darts at waist, perfectly straight, tying the sash with a large bow and ends at the side. A pleated over-skirt can be added at the 18" hip-line to hem, covering the top edge with the sash.

FIRST WORLD WAR PERIOD 1914–1918. Long dresses with sashes and belt at normal waist-line. Artificial flowers at waist-line or shoulder—sometimes both. Short gathered or flared peplums and flounces could be added from the waist, under the sash, straight all-round, at 18" length, or alternatively dipping at the back. Long tight sleeves should be worn. The long dresses could be used underneath lace over-robes. These should be cut with a normal waist-line, either gathered or flared from the waist, with long plain, or gathered topped sleeves over the bare arm. A bishop sleeve was also worn in this period, this being either gathered or plain at the head, and gathered at the wrist into a 1" fitted band.

ROMAN AND GRECIAN PERIODS. Using the sleeveless long dresses adding a draped tabard or over-dress of the same or contrasting material, gathered at shoulders only, with a girdle or belt around the waist to hold the fullness. The tabards are made either with a one shoulder effect, cut from neck-line on one shoulder diagonally to waist, back and front, on the opposite side caught at waist with girdle or sash, or wide gold or silver belt. The belts look very lovely if covered with coloured stones. These costumes could also be worn as modern evening gowns in up-to-date plays.

For medieval period use long dresses, darted to shape at waist, with long loose sleeves, narrow or beaded girdles, attached at 2″ below waist, crossing and dropping at front to the hem of the garment.

The basic dresses should be made in a moss crepe, or satin backed crepe. Best of all in silk or fine wool jersey, which do not crease, and travel well. Stockinette, in both wool and artificial silk is quite cheap and makes up well, but has a tendency to crease, but the creases come out easily if the material is pressed on the wrong side with a warm iron. This dress does not make up well in taffeta or cotton.

CAPES. Very full flared capes are good stock, as they can be used for overskirts. If made double, in the same material, or lined with another colour, they make a reversible cape or skirt. When made single the capes should not have a deep hem but be finely machined all round, or better still hand rolled. As a skirt a cape looks well when draped at one side, with flowers trailing. Capes of only 45″ in length could be used as skirts. Full length capes could not be used in this way.

Hooped Underskirt (Crinoline) and Pads

A Victorian crinoline, size 3 yards at hem, 2 yards at waist, 33″ in length.

Cut a piece of unbleached calico one yard long by one yard four inches wide, fold on the double with the yard length downwards from waist to hem. At the waist mark 6″ from the centre, at the hem 9″ from the centre, leaving $1\frac{1}{2}$″ for turn-up at top and bottom. Then mark lines across at 11″ intervals, from waist to hem, which will divide the skirt into three parts. There will now be four lines across (including waist and hem). Number these lines from the waist downwards—1, 2, 3, and 4. At No. 2 line mark $7\frac{1}{2}$″ across, at No. 3 line 8″ across, then with the yardstick connect these marks into a diagonal line from waist to hem. When cutting leave 1″ seam. Cut six pieces like this, open them out, seam them together, and leave on one seam only 11″ opening which will be the back. Hem each side of the opening, strengthening the bottom with tape.

Machine top and bottom hems and sew 1″ tape across lines 2 and 3 for slotting, using double tape for strength and leaving openings on the back seam.

Cut three lengths of $\frac{1}{2}$″ or $\frac{3}{4}$″ steel—the piece for No. 2 line to measure two yards and that for No. 3 line two yards and twelve inches, and for No. 4 line (the hem) three yards. Seal the ends of the steel with cellotape or adhesive tape, before slotting into the correct lines.

The waist should now measure two yards, through which slot a tape, draw up to the size required, and tie at the back opening.

To get the required lengths of steel, bend backwards and forwards until it snaps. Leave 1″ either side for overlapping.

After slotting the steel into the hoop, bind the overlap—1″—with tape, and sew very strongly over the join, otherwise the hoop may collapse at the wrong moment.

SIDE PADS. Cut a piece of calico 9″ long by 6″ wide and mark a semi-circle on one side. Leave opening on the straight side (which is the waist). Stuff with shredded wadding. Machine 1″ seam at waist and attach—one each side—to a tape to tie in front.

BACK PADS. The method is the same as for the side pads, except that the size should be 12″ in length and 8″ in width attaching the centre of the pads to a tape to tie in front.

A FARTHINGALE. A padded roll 20″ long by 6″ wide. Seam the long edges together to make a tube, gather one of the ends firmly, stuff with shredded wadding until very full, gather remaining end and attach tape on either side, to tie in front.

The Restoration and the Georgian hooped skirt is made in the same way as the Victorian, except for the waist. Here it is necessary to make a tight foundation under-skirt, fitting the waist and hips, with a 12″ opening at the back. Gather the material at the waist leaving 6″ plain back and front. This will necessitate gathers at the sides only. Attach the side hip pads to the gathered part, putting the centre of the pad to the exact centre of the side, attach the tight foundation garment to the underneath of the hoop, then fix the waist on to a 1″ petersham band.

At each side of the 6″ plain space back and front, sew downwards on to the undergarment, so attaching them together, and this will keep the front and back flat and allow the sides to bulge.

EDWARDIAN SKIRT. Lay material double, right side inside. When cutting leave 1″ seams and 3″ at hem. Use yardstick to mark seams. Freehand curved lines at hem.

Centre Front Panel. Waist from centre to side front seam 4″. Centre front fold to hem 40″. Side front seam 43″. Round hem 16″.

Side Panel. Waist 6″. Side front seam 43″. Side back seam 48″. Round hem 34″.

Back Panel. Waist 9″. Side back seam 48″. Centre back seam 54″. Round hem 38″.

Balance marks on all seams at 9″ down from waist.

Placket opening at centre back 11″ down from waist.

S.F. Tack seams on front panel to S.F. seams on side panel, then S.B. seams on side panel to S.B. seams on back panel. Lastly centre back seam leaving placket opening. Make sure balance marks match on all seams.

44

Inverted pleat from 3″ to C.B. then 1″ space and another 3″ pleat towards the inverted one at C.B. This skirt can be used with a jacket or as the bottom half of a dress.

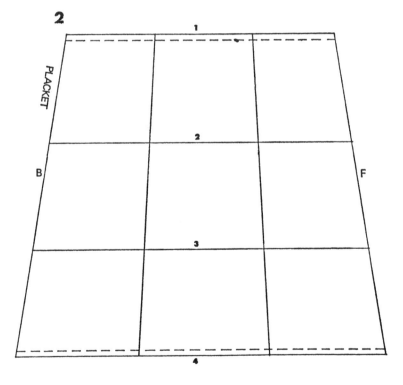

Fig. 3. Victorian hooped petticoat. Flat (2) and made up (1).

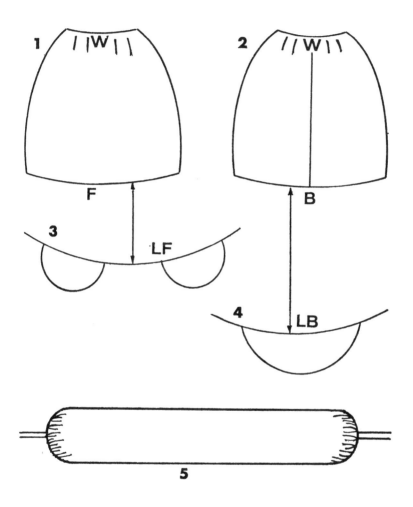

Fig. 4. Restoration and Georgian foundation underskirt (1 and 2). Side pads (3). Back pad (4). Farthingale (5).

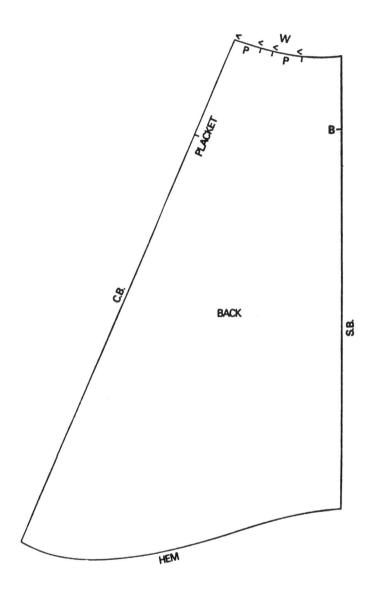

Fig. 5. Edwardian skirt pattern. Back panels.

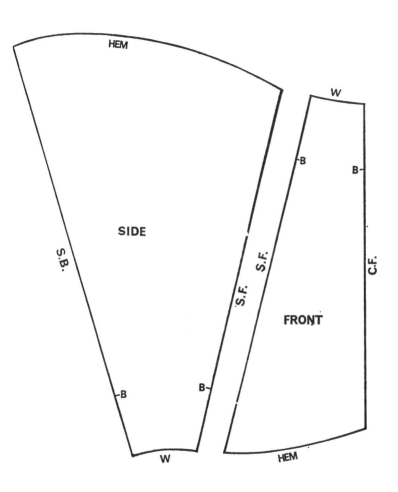

Fig. 6. Edwardian skirt pattern. Front and side panels.

Maintenance Care and Storage of Costumes, etc.

There should be a large airy room available for storage in which should be some moveable dress rails, on wheels, a chest of drawers and shelves, also a skip which is a theatrical costume basket with lid, and some boxes. Dress rails can be bought from shop outfitters—Messrs. Pollard of Old Street, E.C.1—others can be found in the classified telephone directory. If the rails are too expensive to buy probably a carpenter or handyman in the company could fix up some suitable rods.

After use the costumes should be thoroughly examined for wear and tear. If the make up around the neck and other staining is slight, remove with a cleaning fluid, but if excessive the costumes should be sent to a dry cleaners; but first see that all repairs are attended to.

There are several cleaning fluids on the market, but 'Beaucaire' is one that is highly recommended and the best way to use it is as follows. Place a few folded sheets of tissue paper under the garment at the position of the stain and using a pad of tissue paper soaked with the fluid rub briskly with a circular motion until the stain grows fainter, then moving the position of the paper underneath repeat the process until the mark has disappeared. Only use tissue paper on wool, cotton and other hard surfaced materials, not on silks, satins, and other delicate fabrics, as it is obvious that the paper would scratch the surface. Instead use a pad of cotton wool or wadding when cleaning these latter materials.

See that all hooks, eyes, and patent fasteners are sewn on securely and all split seams, tears, lace, etc., are mended. Then put the garment on a shoulder hanger. If it is a full length ladies' gown see that loops of tape are sewn at the waist, which can then be put on the shoulder hanger. Hangers with notches are obtainable, but if using wire ones turn up the ends when the garment will not fall off.

It is imperative for dress shields to be sewn into the armholes of all clothes. They can be bought in all sizes and are available for men, but if men's dress shields are difficult to come by, use the largest size in women's. The chief asset in having dress shields is that when they are soiled they are easily replaceable, thus saving garments from being spoilt.

White collars, cuffs and trimmings should be removed and washed, and if not replaced on costumes, stored between sheets of tissue paper, in a drawer or box kept for that purpose.

When costumes are ready for storage, cover with a plastic or unbleached calico cover, pinning the bottoms of the cover up envelope fashion and securing with pins. Plastic covers are sold in stores and markets. For a calico cover take two pieces of material 27″ wide by 62″ long, seam together leaving the hem open and a small opening at the top for the hanger to go through.

The calico covers should be washed periodically and the plastic replaced with new ones from time to time.

Never store garments which are dirty or in need of repair, thinking that they can be cleaned when required, as the dirt can become so ingrained as to be irremovable, also dirt invites insects. The old adage 'A stitch in time saves nine' was never truer.

Always endeavour to store an immaculate costume.

Woollen jumpers, leotards and tights need to be laid flat in a skip or drawer, between sheets of newspaper.

Hats, etc., should be filled out with tissue paper, covered and pinned up in brown paper and stored flat on shelves. Anti-moth crystals called 'Paradichlorbenzine' (P.O.B.) and camphor balls are sold by the pound in chemists.

Make small bags, about 2″ square, in which put some crystals or a few camphor balls, then sew a tape loop on one corner to hang on each shoulder hanger before storing clothes. Sprinkle the crystals or place camphor balls between the woollens on the sheets of newspaper before closing the lids of skips or drawers, and put bags of the crystals, etc., between the hats on the shelves.

Periodically look at the clothes and brush them and keep some Flit or D.D.T. handy for spraying each month in the summer and three monthly in the winter on to each side of the covers.

To store shoes, etc., buy cheap shoe trees for them and keep the footwear polished and brushed, in boxes or on shelves, paired and tied together as nothing is more frustrating than looking for a missing shoe when urgently required. These precautions may sound arduous but must be maintained if the wardrobe is to be preserved.

Some Facts on Period Clothes

In the first place men and women wore the furs of animals which they had killed.

Centuries later when people had learnt to spin and weave, clothes were made from flax and wool. These were simple tunics for both men and women, to which were added lengths of material across the shoulders, as shawls and cloaks. These materials were dyed with vegetable dyes to make a variety of colours.

The Romans and Greeks wore splendid draped tunics with cloaks and togas over them. The military men wore a leather and metal type of jerkin over their tunics, with cloaks according to rank.

The Greeks

Materials used were wool of coarse and fine loose weave which draped well, also linens in coarse and fine transparent weaves. Silk was very rare in those days. Borders of embroidery edged tunics and robes, in geometric and trailing leaf designs. The garments worn were called 'Chitons'. The men's robes were named 'Ionian Chitons' and the women's 'Dorian' or 'Doric Chitons'. These were pieces of material, about a half yard longer than the height of the person, folded back at the shoulder, allowing the extra material to show, and caught at the neck with an ornamental pin. The styles were varied by the wearing of girdles, belts or sashes, and the material could be plain with embroidered hem, or dyed all over with small spots or flowers.

Tight chitons of fancy woven wools were also fashionable, and very draped chitons cut much longer than required, tucked up over a fine cord and very much bloused. Short chitons were worn over long ones, which when draped created a peplum or flounce.

Young men favoured short draped chitons, which sometimes were cut with one shoulder free, over which were cloaks called 'Chlamys' which consisted of an oblong piece of material, 2 yards long by $1\frac{1}{4}$ yards wide. This was caught at the neck with an ornament or pin, and worn plain or bordered with embroidery, and draped around the shoulders.

Older men wore longer chitons at mid-calf or ankle length. A shawl or 'Hymation' was a large rectangular piece of material varying from three to four yards in length and in width (from the wearer's under-arm to ankle) averaging one and a half to two yards. The cloth was draped from the left armpit in the front, under the right armpit and round the back, over the left shoulder, across the front over the right shoulder and across the back, with any surplus material hanging over the left arm. This made a kind of upwards spiral sweep twice across the body. The hymation was worn over both the short and long chitons. If worn alone, a loin cloth would be necessary underneath. Nowadays, for theatrical purposes, the hymation could be made in fine wool, jersey, or towelling. When Sir Ralph Richardson joined a film company in Greece a year or so ago, he took his own wardrobe of Greek classic costumes—made in England especially to his own requirements, in fine white towelling, some dyed a natural shade, and in the finished film the material looked as if it had been hand woven. The Greek women wore outer garments also called 'Hymations' and 'Chlamys', the former being draped around the waist, over the shoulder (not under the armpit as in the case of the men). The chlamy was worn exactly the same as the men, caught at the neck with a brooch or pin. It could also be worn around the shoulders and over the arms as a stole or shawl.

When draping the hymation for a woman it is best to commence at the left side of the waist, over the left arm, then twice around the waist, allowing the surplus to drape at the left side in a waterfall effect.

The Greeks went mostly barefoot but sometimes wore simple sandals laced up the leg.

The men's hair was worn long and kept out of the eyes with a flat head-band. Later on the hair was cut shorter and bound with a narrow ribbon.

The women wore their hair very long in a knot or bun at the nape of the neck, caught with an ornament. Hats as we know them were never seen, but the hymation could always be draped over the head to provide a covering.

Suitable materials for use in this period. Men and women: Woollen crepe, afghalaine, wool and silk jersey, stockinette, Viyella, thin flannel, towelling, linen, noile, lawn and cotton voile.

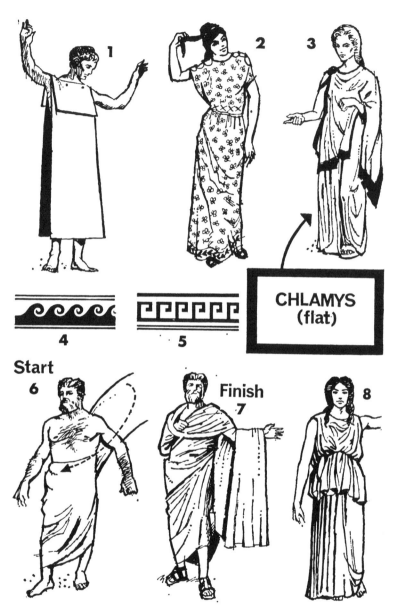

CHLAMYS
(flat)

Start

Finish

Fig. 7. G REEK: 1 Ionian chiton. 2 Doric chiton. 3 Chlamys (worn). 4 and 5 Types of embroidery. 6 and 7 Hymation (how to drape). 8 Doric chiton with peplum.

The Romans

The materials were similar to those used by the Greeks—wools and linens—but some of the royal togas and tunicas were made of a coarse material woven in pure silk (not flax) but similar to linen in appearance. The tunica was like the cotton chiton worn by the Greeks comprising two rectangualr pieces, sewn at shoulders and sides, leaving the neck and armholes free, or cut in one long piece, with a slit for the head, joined from the under-arm to hem, leaving space for the arms. Could also be worn with one shoulder free, by putting one arm over the shoulder of the tunica, instead of under. A girdle or belt was worn around the waist which allowed the top part to blouse over. There were varied lengths for these tunicas—above or below the knee, or full ankle length. Later on sleeves were added and in the case of some older men, long wrist length sleeves. When Mr Rex Harrison appeared in the Cleopatra film the costumiers supplied a special wardrobe, designed by Mr Nino Noverese. In the finished film Mr Harrison—who played Julius Ceasar—wore a purple robe pleated from neck to ankles, which had long sleeves pleated round the arm, and this outfit was not in the original wardrobe. After the initial surprise it was felt that this outfit added to Mr Harrison's performance, as he was playing an older man, and gave dignity and stature to his part. The other men around him had bare arms and knees, and in this new tunica, worn with a purple toga, he certainly looked magnificent.

The tunicas were sometimes trimmed with vertical bands of purple or red material, back and front, and trailing leaf patterns in gold or silver were embroidered on to these bands, with edgings of gold or silver braid. A royal tunica would have a red or purple panel measuring 10″ to 12″, down the centre front, with an embroidered leaf design in gold or silver on both sides of the panel, and the royal crest in gold on the front. The under-garment to these tunicas was a loin cloth, shaped and worn as a baby's napkin is at the present time. The toga was an oblong piece of material—similar to the Greek hymation—5 yards by 2 yards. Could be cut in a semi-circle, the straight edge 5 yards long and in the widest part across 2 yards, worn plain, sometimes bordered with bands of mauve or red, with gold or silver leaf embroidery and matching braids as in the tunica.

On religious and ceremonial occasions the toga was worn over the head. Royal togas in red or purple had trailing patterns embroidered all over them, in gold or silver and on ceremonial occasions, when these were worn with the royal tunicas, gold or silver laurels were worn on the head.

Togas could also be folded two or three times lengthwise, until they were about 18″ wide and were then worn across the left shoulder at the back dropping on the right to about the knee, and up again to the left shoulder, with the surplus material hanging down the back. When a toga was worn alone a loin cloth was underneath.

Laced and slatted boots called 'Calcaeus' were worn by Roman citizens, but royal calcaeus were embroidered with leaf designs and trimmed with animal heads appliqued in leather. Other footwear were sandals called 'Solea', comprising a leather sole with lacing up the leg.

Ornaments of lion and animal heads were fashionable.

The men used a travelling cloak with a hood called a 'Paenula', which was a semi-circular piece of heavy woollen material, or leather, open down the front and fastened at the neck with a leather thong or ornament. The paenula could also be worn thrown over the shoulders, hanging down the back, and leaving the front free.

The men went mainly bareheaded, the hair cut short and brushed forward with a fringe at the forehead.

Wreaths of real laurel and bay leaves were often worn, but the gold wreaths were copied from these and were only worn by royalty (sometimes by generals). Julius Caesar always appeared in a laurel wreath.

The Roman women wore robes in the manner of the Greek chiton, ankle length and draped at the waist on to a girdle, often with an embroidered hem. These garments were called 'Stolas'.

Made in fine wool or silk imported from the east, the colours were in vivid hues, rather than pastel shades. The undergarment was called a 'Tunica Interior', of a fine soft linen or muslin. The early Roman women wore togas similar to the men. This was later discarded and replaced with an oblong shawl, 4 yards by 2 yards called the 'Palla', worn in the same style as the Greek hymation. A palla $1\frac{1}{2}$ yards square could be draped from the left shoulder under the right armpit, back to the left shoulder and caught with an ornament, plain or embroidered materials being used.

Solea were on the feet and calcaeus in a softer leather than those of the men, and gayer colours were favoured.

The hair styles were like those of the Greek ladies at first, but became more elaborate as the years went by. The hair plaited and coiled on the top of the head in the form of a coronet, false hair was used trimmed with elaborate bands and ribbons. The hair was also plaited in with ribbons in bright colours.

The royal ladies wore coronets and crowns in gold, encrusted with precious stones.

Suitable materials for use in this period. Similar to the Greeks, but add velour and facecloth.

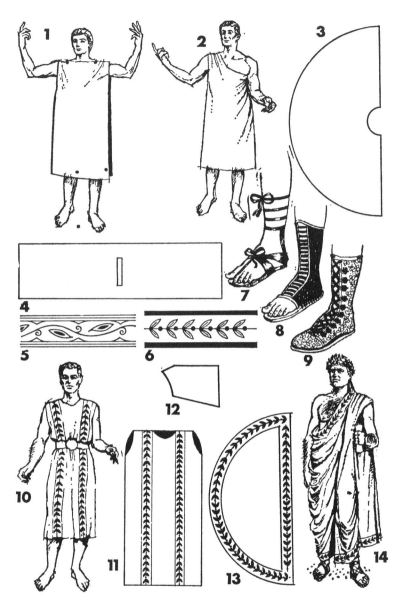

Fig. 8. ROMAN: 1 Tunica. 2 Tunica worn underarm. 3 Paenula. 4 Tunica (flat). 5 and 6 Types of embroidery. 7 Sandal. 8 and 9 Two types of boots. 10 Tunica with bands of embroidery (worn). 11 The same as 10 (flat). 12 Hood to attach to paenula. 13 Toga (flat). 14 Toga (worn draped).

Saxons and Normans

(The word in inverted commas denotes the name by which the garment was known in the period)

The usual attire for the men was linen under-tunics, 'Shertes', similar to the collarless shirts of today, over which was a knee-length garment of linen or wool (mostly with long sleeves). Some of the tunics were parti-coloured, i.e. one half of a different colour from the other and plain and figured materials were used in this manner. The tunics were slashed into strips or tacets 2″ wide, from knee to hem, over which were 'Clokes' varying in length, draped on to one shoulder and drawn through a ring-shaped buckle. Sleeveless surcoats, 'Cyclas', were worn over full-sleeved tunics and these were slit in front to the knee, with the sides left open from armhole to hem and caught in three or four places with buttons which could be adjusted for riding. Later on in this period cyclas had sleeves and hoods added with fur or sheepskin linings. Legs were covered in 'Braccos', loose fitting and cross gartered with strips of leather or coarse webbing. Boots were shaped to the feet, buckled with an ankle strap or buttoned. Other boots were just 'pull-ons' and fitted round the ankles.

The nobility wore tunics and clokes of rich materials, embroidered around the neck, sleeves and hem, and sometimes fur-trimmed. Velvet clokes, both long and short were fashionable and tighter braccos (similar to the tights of today) with one leg of a different colour from the other, or one striped and one plain leg.

The poorer classes were clothed in simple tunics and clokes in harsh heavy wools, homespuns and hand-made tweeds, in dull colours, with woollen braccos, hose made of cloth and the feet bare. When footwear was necessary a stout leather boot was buckled and strapped across the instep.

The shoes were of soft leather, in a variety of colours, hair was rather long and simple and beards of all types, and moustaches were favoured.

Hats were small and of a conical shape, and in the case of the

61

Fig. 9. SAXON: 1 and 2 'Cyclas'. 3 Tunic (short). 4 Tunic (long). 5 Dipped sleeve (flat). 6 Dipped sleeve (worn). 7 Conical hat. 8 Hood. 9 Boot with anklestrap. 10 'Braccos'. 11 Pull-on boot. 12 Cloke.

nobility headwear was of gold headbands and crowns encrusted with precious stones.

The women were clothed in long chemises of fine linen over which were long flowing gowns, 'Gunnes', with trains varying from one to two yards. The materials were wool, heavy raw silk and velvets. Sleeves were long and tight, or tight to the elbow then falling to the hem of the dress.

Another variation was a three-quarter length tunic, bordered with fur, worn over a long skirt, the wide three-quarter length sleeve of the tunic having a fur cuff, and worn over a long tight sleeve. When fur was not used, heavily braided and embroidered bands were substituted.

The clokes were similar in shape and style to those of the men, but there was a full circular one, with a hole for the head, which dipped in length from the hips at front to the ankles at the back.

Stockings were made of both wool and cloth, gartered at the knee and shoes were flat, similar to those of the men. Headscarves were draped under the chin and over the shoulders, concealing the hair, but sometimes a long plait of hair intertwined with ribbons, was shown on each side of the face. The ladies of the nobility wore gold crowns and circlets, set with precious stones, around the forehead, over the headscarves, also jewelled girdles and sashes trailing to the ankles.

The poorer class wore coarse linen chemises with shorter overgowns of rough wool with long sleeves and waist-line belts into which the hem of the over-robe could be tucked when working.

The colours were drab.

The head covering was either a linen hood with a hole for the face, or a headscarf wound around the head and tied under the chin.

The cloth stockings were gartered under the knee, and the footwear was in the form of small boots. Many went barefoot.

Suitable materials for use in this period. Repp (both cotton and woollen) wool jersey, tweed, frieze, damask, brocade, velvet, satin, chiffon, lawn, batiste.

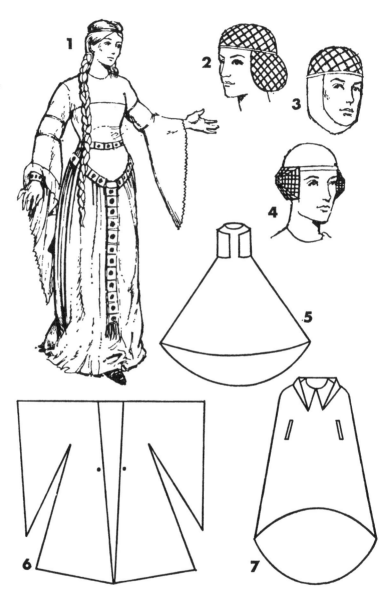

Fig. 10. NORMAN: 1 Gunne. 2 Crespinette. 3 Coif with Barbette. 4 Reticuled head-dress. 5 Sideless gunne. 6 Eastern surcoat. 7 Pelicon.

Gothic Period

Men's medieval costumes underwent a change. Ankle length sleeveless under-robes, 'Shertes', were worn over which were short knee-length tunics, 'Bliauts'. These were cut at the waist into two parts, the upper being a high-necked bodice with sleeves cut in one piece (the shape that today is called 'Magyar'). The skirts varied in style. One was cut in two semi-circular pieces to reach the knee, seamed at the sides, then pleated into the waist. Another was cut ankle length at the back, rising at the front to the knee, and left open back and front, from the waist, with bands of embroidery on either side of the openings. As an alternative bands of embroidery were sometimes placed horizontally about 8" from the waist and around the hem.

Bodices were also trimmed with these bands of embroidery at the neck and bottoms of the sleeves.

Sleeves in bliauts were either full or close-fitting at the wrist, but armholes were always cut very deep, almost to the waist.

There was also a straight tunic, 'Cotte', high necked and tied with a girdle round the waist which enabled the front of the skirt to be draped over the girdle thus revealing more of the under garment. These girdles were from 1" to 2" in width, made of leather, gilded and painted, or in silk with embroidery and set with stones.

Separate embroidered collars of varied shapes were sometimes worn on the plain neck of the cottes. The sleeves were similar to those of the bliauts.

Circular clokes of wool were also worn over these garments fixed at the neck with an ornament, also a square piece of wool, called a 'Pallium', the latter being draped over the left shoulder and tied at the waist on the opposite side.

At this time parti-coloured tunics and tights were fashionable, and sometimes one leg was striped with the other plain.

Later in this period clothes became more elaborate. The under-tunics had long tight sleeves, buttoned to the elbow, over which

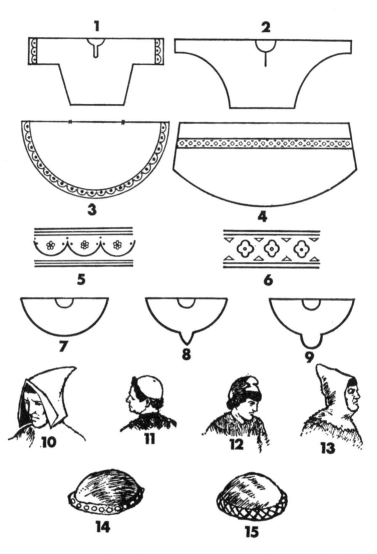

Fig. 11. GOTHIC: 1 Bliant (short sleeves and shaped skirt, 1 and 3). 2 Bliant (long sleeves and gathered skirt, 2 and 4). 5 and 6 Types of embroidery. 7, 8 and 9 Three types of collars. 10 Hood. 11 Skull cap. 12 Conical cap. 13 Conical hood. 14 and 15 Flat hats.

was a 'cyclas' (a sleeveless garment scolloped all round the edge) and lined with a contrasting colour, and having a large scolloped edged draped collar. A doublet called a 'Pourpoint' was now in fashion, made in embroidered and brocaded materials, either worn short or to the knee according to taste. The collar was invariably high, the sleeves varied from long and tight to dipping at the wrist to about mid-calf. Another version of the sleeve had a hole in the centre about elbow length where the arm came through shewing a tight under-sleeve, leaving the surplus of the outer sleeve hanging down to the hem of the doublet. There were also circular mantles, with or without hoods, with no opening at the front, but with holes for the head and arms, which were worn in three ways. Either in the normal fashion from neck to ankles, or draped on one shoulder revealing one arm, the third way being draping all fullness up to the neck in front and letting it all flow over the shoulder down the back.

These clokes were cut with front openings and caught at neck, and several times down the front with ornaments.

Another garment was a 'Houppelande', a long full-skirted outer robe with high collar and flowing sleeves with scolloped edges. The length of the 'Houppelande' and the width and length of the sleeves varied to suit the wearer's tastes. It was made in heavy brocaded materials.

There was also another outer garment called a 'Pelicon' in heavy wool or velvet, fur lined, and with or without a hood.

Cloke tunics were outer garments open each side of the front, thus leaving a loose panel in the centre front which was belted, thus leaving the cloke free at sides and back.

Hose was tighter and well tailored, made in wool, silk or velvet, sometimes footless and strapped under the sole, at other times, as stockings, complete with feet. Pouches slung on a strap from the shoulder, 'Gipseres', in leather and materials were worn. Sometimes these pouches were attached to belts.

There were hoods of a conical shape with holes for the face, fitted over the shoulders in front for comfort, the point at the top hanging over the back of the head. Small flat-topped skull caps and hats and small round hats on which were draped pieces of material to hang over the shoulder.

Other types of headwear were hoods in various forms. Some worked on to a hat brim 'Roundel' draped in many ways, and worn over the shoulder.

With pointed ear-pieces (similar to jesters).

With one long end two yards in length called 'Liripipe' draped over one shoulder and tucked into a belt, or draped around the head giving the appearance of a turban. Later on men wore the hair in page-boy style to the shoulder or cut short at the back with the front hair rolled. With this style of hair were worn small pill-box hats, 5″ in height narrowing at the top, and brimmed hats the draped crowns of which had a long end hanging across the shoulder like the liripipe.

The footwear consisted of very pointed flat shoes, in leather or material, with more elaborate styles decorated in gold and jewels. Also calf length boots in soft kid. Shoes of felt and wooden shoes similar to clogs, was the footwear of the poorer classes who also had much simpler tunics, and hose in drab wools.

The women's medieval costumes also underwent a change. For the first time gowns, 'bliauts', were cut in two parts with a low waist-line bodice and separate skirts. Around the bodice was a corsage, draped in a mid-riff effect from under bust to hip from which hung a full gathered skirt. Over the corsage was a long girdle which tied around the hip and dropped to the hem. The girdle was 2″ wide, embroidered or beaded and had tassled or fringed ends.

Sleeves were cut full, set into a normal armhole, which was appearing for the first time. A popular style was made in soft material finely crimped. This crimping, called 'Treebark', can be done nowadays by pleating firms, several of which work for theatrical costumiers.

The crimped bliaut bodices were cut very high waisted, actually only a yoke just below the armhole, with the skirts flowing therefrom. With this style the girdle was worn around the waist, then around the hips, hanging down the centre front.

There were semi-circular clokes in wools and velvets, collarless

68

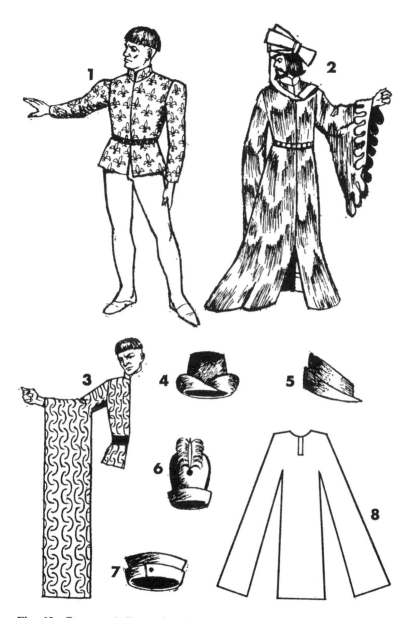

Fig. 12. GOTHIC: 1 Pourpoint. 2 Houppeland with roundel on head. 3 Pourpoint with dropping sleeve. 4, 5, 6 and 7 Four varied hats. 8 Cloke tunic.

or with small flat collars. These clokes did not meet in the front, but a space of 3″ was left with a cord attached to each side. A more elaborate garment was made in brocade and damask.

An unusual garment from the East, a 'surcoat', made its appearance. It was loose, made in a thin or transparent silk, with large flowing sleeves hanging in points to the knees. This was caught at the waist with an ornament, or could be worn with a girdle around the waist. This surcoat which became very popular was later made in heavier materials.

The hair, when seen, was in long plaits, or braids with narrow headbands circling the forehead. At other times the plaits were coiled on each side of the head.

Headwear became a fashion and there were several styles— the 'Coif', the 'Crespinette' and the 'Gorget'.

The 'Coif' was either a small pill-box or cap worn on top of the head over a flat piece of material caught under the chin 'Barbette'.

Crespinette was a trellised cap with snood attached, worn over a barbette.

The Gorget was a draped piece of material caught on to the side plaits then draped into the neck of the gown, thus leaving the top of the head bare. If required, a flat pill-box or cap could be worn with this.

Later in the period sleeveless gowns which were open and laced at the sides, were worn over ones of contrasting colours, with long sleeves.

A popular garment was a sideless gown, which was cut with a large opening from shoulder to hip, on each side, worn over another of a contrasting colour, with long sleeves.

A sleeveless pelicon, cut with a long train, with openings for head and arms, attached to which was a hood which folded back into a collar when not worn on the head.

The clokes were made from velvet and brocade and cut with such long trains (lined with vivid contrasting satins) that it was necessary for a page to hold them up. Some neck-lines on gowns were being cut rather low and boat-shape in line, edged with bands of embroidery and jewels, shewing the tops of the arms.

The bands of embroidery were repeated in the hip-line. Head-dresses were more elaborate. 'Reticuled' head-dresses had trel-lised cages over each ear with veilings draped over.

A conical shape 'Hennian' or wimple had veiling draped from the point.

Another style was a padded roll around the head with trellised gold braid in the centre, sewn with pearls, veiling hanging from the back of the head and a barbette attached under the chin from side to side.

A 'Corse' or corset of soft leather, or a stiff material, laced in front, was a foundation garment.

Women's shoes for the most part were concealed, but very pointed heelless shoes of soft leather were worn.

Gloves were becoming fashionable for men and women. Short gauntlet style, with some embroidered and scolloped at the cuff edge, in soft leathers for the ladies and stouter leathers for the men. For riding and hawking there were longer gauntlets, lined with sheepskin, or a flat haired fur.

Working class garments were in a rough harsh heavy wool, homespuns and hand made tweeds in subdued shades. Footwear was of stout hardwearing leather, and clogs. Mittens, 'Moufle', were worn by workers, which kept the hands warm but left the fingers free.

Suitable materials for use in this period. Velvet, brocade, fur-cloths, wool and silk jersey, damask, stockinette, organza, linen, poplin, velour, facecloth, frieze, afghalaine, leathers, suede cloth, gold painted cottons (Burnet's), organdi, cotton voile, chiffon, gold and silver American cloth.

Tudor Period

In the earlier years the men wore short tunics—called 'Paltocks'—both braided and embroidered, over which were worn contrasting surcoats, both long and short.

The tunics were waist length, cut with a low 'V' neck to the waist, and laced across. There were others with full padded skirts to the knees, the skirts or 'Bases' were detachable at the waist, and semi-circular in shape.

The padding was done in a series of corrugations from waist to hem, caught with braid at the back, or on to a foundation lining. The bases were open at the back, and if used for riding made with open fronts.

The sleeves of the period were varied. One style was puffed at the head where the top of the sleeve met the shoulder then gathered above the elbow, and fitted into a tight cuff to the wrist. Another type was open at the head and elbow, with contrasting material, puffed out in both these places. Double sleeves were also worn which consisted of a short elbow length sleeve over a tight-fitting long one. There were slashed sleeves with contrasting colours showing through.

The under-shirts were of white linen, the neck-lines being full, either tucked or gathered, sleeves being full both at head and wrist, collars and cuffs and edgings of black embroidery—called 'Spanish Work'.

Surcoats were in wool or heavy brocade and velvet, with turned back revers of contrasting materials, or large fur collars. Some were trimmed with fur. The surcoats were either sleeveless or had long sleeves puffed at head and wrist. Others were wide at the wrist with fur cuffs. There were three lengths, to hip, knee or ankle. As an alternative to the surcoat there was a specially shaped cloak, circular in front, open from neck and dipping to a point at the centre back. The neck was circular and in the centre back there was a slit from waist to hem. When used for riding it was worn in the normal way—over the shoulders and arms.

When required for other occasions it was arranged over the left shoulder around the chest, leaving the right shoulder exposed.

This cloak was made in wool with contrasting borders and lined with silk, but for wet weather it was made in felt.

Tight 'hosen' were worn on the legs with 'cod pieces', the latter being padded (in the form of a small shaped cushion), attached to the crotch of the hosen.

Leather or material pouches attached to belts were sometimes worn.

The hair was worn long, sometimes to the shoulders. Some hats were in fleecy felts (referred to as 'Beaver') having large brims sweeping up to one side, trimmed with plumes, and others were small and made in velvet, one particular shape having an upturned brim cut into battlements, trimmed with small feather tips trailing over the brim and down to the ear.

The footwear comprised square toed shoes and boottees, some with slashed toecaps with contrasting colours showing through. 'Pedules' were high boots of soft leather, either plain or with turned back cuffs of contrasting leather.

Workmen and peasants were clothed in coarse linen shirts under tunics, or jerkins and capes of rough wool. Loose cloth hosen caught at the knee and ankles with cords. Skull caps with small felt hats over them, or hoods under felt hats. Belts with pouches of leather. Thick and heavy shoes and boots. The hair was not as long as the gentry.

The women at this time had gowns cut separate at the waistline, with fitted bodices with high and low neck-lines. The skirts were very full. The materials used were rich brocades and velvets.

The skirts were so heavy that they were lifted in front to enable the wearer to walk freely, or draped over the arm. Another way of the skirt being lifted was a button being attached at the back of the waist where a loop sewn at the hem of the skirt would hang from, showing the richness of the petticoat underneath.

Voluminous petticoats of pleated muslin and cambric, with frills of embroidery. At this time an embroidery called 'Cut Work' was making its appearance, which is what we now call 'Broderie Anglaise', then made entirely by hand of cut out

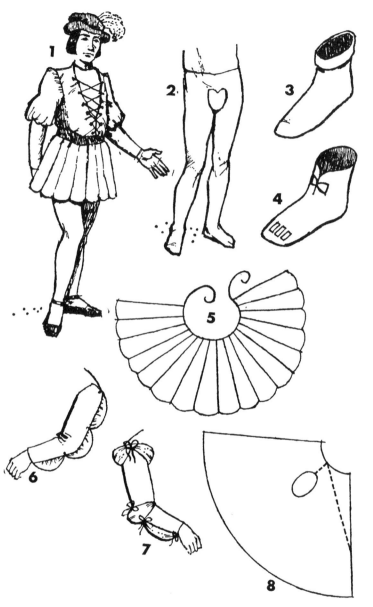

Fig. 13. TUDOR: 1 Tunic and paltock with bonet on head. 2 Hosen with codepiece. 3 and 4 Pedules. 5 Paltock (detachable). 6 and 7 Two types of sleeves. 8 Sleeveless surcoat.

flower patterns oversewn with a whipping or button hole stitch.

Another embroidery was cut out patterns of linen appliqued on to net.

Sleeves varied, some being very full, dipping to a point, others with turned back cuffs of contrasting material, or double sleeves being full and short over tight under-sleeves. Another variation was a long puff sleeve caught at the elbow and wrists with gathering.

Cloaks were of velvet or brocade with satin or fur linings. There were also square shawls and long stoles.

The head-dresses were of a spanish type. A 'gable' head-dress in wool or velvet was very much in favour. This had a border of embroidery and was stiffened at the edge to form a gable point at the top of the head. Another type of head-wear was in wool or velvet semi-circular in shape and worn turned back over the forehead to show a contrasting colour.

The ladies of the nobility wore coronets over their head-dresses.

Shoes were flat, with or without ankle straps.

Many jewels were worn in the form of brooches, rings and necklaces.

The country and working women had very drab clothes in rough wool. Bodices were laced and had square necks, the under-shifts showing through were frilled at the neck. The skirts were double, the upper one rolled back into a belt when working. The straight cut sleeves were also rolled back when working.

The head-wear consisted of either little turned-back caps tied under the chin or kerchiefs of white linen tied around the head, showing no hair.

White cotton aprons and detachable white cotton over-sleeves buttoned on to the sleeves of the gown were sometimes worn. The shoes were stout leather, plain or with ankle straps.

In the late Tudor period the men's costumes were very elaborate tunics and bases being decorated with much gold braiding and embroideries. Sleeves became very full with lots of slashings, also very puffed and caught with buttons.

Surcoats were fuller and pleated. One surcoat called a 'Chamarre' which was adapted from a French fashion, was a

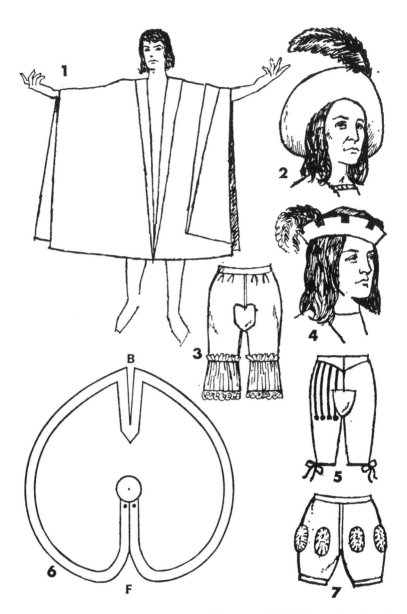

Fig. 14. TUDOR: 1 Chamarre. 2 Hat with upturned brim (Beaver). 3, 5 and 7 Cut hosen or knee breeches. 4 Bonet. 6 Circular cloke suitable for riding.

square mantle, the sides being folded back on to the shoulder, having a large square collar. It was made in rich materials and lined in a way as to make it reversible.

Cut hosen now made their appearance which were knee breeches with vertical slashings and embroideries, sometimes on one leg only. Garters were worn and shown. There was not much change in the head-wear, except for one rather popular flat shape made in velvet. This had a flat brim topped by a crown of the same size, with a feather tip at one side falling over the ear. This hat was called a 'Bonet'. The men of fashion wore these bonets embroidered and studded with precious stones and gold ornaments. There was no change in the footwear.

The lower and working classes were wearing knee length tunics and smocks, also simple surcoats and capes, cloth hosen and stout shoes, plain or strapped.

Flat bonets unadorned were worn.

The gowns of the ladies in this late Tudor period had large square necks, framed with embroidered bands or set with precious stones, the lace or frilled edgings just showing inside the neck-line. Bodices were cut to flatten the bust, being stiffened underneath with buckram and canvas. Sleeves were gathered at the wrist. There were double sleeves with gathered lace and muslin ones showing under the loose top sleeve. Other sleeves were full at the head where they joined the bodice, but left loose at the wrist and trimmed with large fur cuffs. The shape of the skirt was flat at the front, very full at the back in gathers and falling from the waist into a train about two yards long. They were open down the centre front showing a plain skirt of contrasting material underneath. Embroidered bands edged these openings and around the waist was a girdle with ornamental fobs hanging in the centre front. These were worn over stiffened petticoats. The gable head-dresses were still fashionable, also a Flemish head-dress called a 'Beguin', the latter being stiffened and turned back framing the face showing the front of the hair, covering the back of the head and shoulders. A French hood in black velvet was also worn well back on top of the head, which had a stiffened cuff, parted in the centre, edged with pearls and beads.

Fig. 15. TUDOR: 1 Gown with parted head-dress. 2, 3 and 4 Three types of sleeves. 5 and 6 Bequin (Flemish head-dress). 7 Bag back hood (snood). 8 Semi-circular head-dress. 9 Gable head-dress.

Sometimes faced with another colour, showing an edging of pleated white lace or pleated gold net. 'A Bag Back Hood' (which was a snood) attached to a cap and tied under the chin was sometimes worn. This was made of a trelliswork weave, with pearls sewn on it.

Hair when shown was severely parted in the centre and knotted into a bun at the back, or worn in a snood.

The working women wore plain linen gowns, with sleeveless bodices laced down the front, under which were blouses with gathered necks and full sleeves. Another bodice was cut with a round neck and kerchiefs were tucked into them. Skirts were full and ankle length, with rows of braid around the hem.

The headwear comprised caps and bonnets, tied under the chin and hiding the hair.

Shoes were plain, and slipped on without fastenings.

Suitable materials for use in this period. Satin, velvet, velveteen, corduroy, velour, facecloth, frieze, wild silk, lace broderie anglaise, linen, brocade, furcloth, fur, gold American cloth, cambric, muslin, chiffon, cotton voile and afghalaine.

Elizabethan Period

Men now wore stiffened doublets in woollen materials and velvets, with high necks, a feature being epaulettes of padded rolls around the top of the armholes. From the waist there was a peplum or basque varying in length. The doublets were either trimmed with rows of braid or decorated by slashings done in several rows with contrasting colours showing through. Figure eight ruffs of varying widths were worn at the high necks. The sleeves were full at the head and also slashed in rows similar to the doublet, with cuffs as the figure eight ruffs. Breeches: 'Venetians' were in vogue, which were knee breeches cut full at the waist, trimmed with slashes (as the doublets) or braided and embroidered in rows, placed either diagonally or vertically across. At the knee there were either bows or rosettes.

Another kind of short breeches, 'Slops', reaching just below the thigh, were cut into straps 2″ to 3″ wide, braided at the edges, gathered at top and bottom, with contrasting colours showing through.

Another variation was a tight knee breech extending from the bottom of the slop to the knee.

Short capes, either adorned with rows of braid or trimmed with slashes around the edges, showing colours through, were lined with satins and brocades. These were worn either collarless or with large rectangular collars. Lace was now fashionable. There were several kinds of hand-made lace edgings used on collars, cuffs, shirts and handkerchiefs.

Stockings were being hand-knitted, in silk and cotton. Garters were worn and shown.

Shoes were still flat and heelless, but lavishly trimmed with bows and rosettes.

Hats in felts and velvets, with high crowns, similar to the bowlers of the present day, were in vogue, either trimmed with feathers or ornaments, or with crowns draped with folds of self material.

Hair was worn long. Moustaches and beards were fashionable, the latter being spade shaped and pointed. There was a double-pointed beard called a 'Swallowtail'.

Ear-rings were worn by fops and dandies.

Working men and tradesmen had plainer clothes in subdued colours, and hard wearing shoes.

The women's gowns at this time were made in velvets and brocades, lavishly embroidered and braided and decorated with pearls and beads. The bodices had dipping points in the fronts, mounted over stomachers, these being of canvas, stiffened and boned. Figure eight ruffs were worn on high necks.

There were also high wired collars of muslin or fine silk, mounted over wire and edged with frills of pointed lace. When the neck of the gown was square, the collar was attached from the front corners and fitted around the back of the neck reaching as high as the top of the head. The front of the dress was left plain, on which many brooches and necklaces rested.

Sleeves were full at the head and pouched in several places down to the wrist. Another variation was an over-sleeve (adapted from an earlier period). This had a hole in the front of the sleeve at the position of the elbow, through which a tight sleeve came through with the remainder of the over-sleeve hanging down from elbow to knee.

Skirts were very full at the waist, worn over hooped under-skirts and side pads, or padded rolls, 'farthingales'. The fullness was concentrated in the sides and back of the skirt leaving the front as flat as possible. Some skirts had pleated and gathered basques and peplums of varied lengths, attached from the waist, thus forming a double skirt.

Stockings—hand-knitted—similar to those of the men were worn, the shoes were not visible under the long gowns, but they were very simple and a small heel was now making its appearance.

The hair styling was mostly upswept, and the headgear was small hats (similar in type to those worn by the men). French hoods were still in favour and there were small caps with heart-shaped brims. Royal ladies and the nobility wore coronets and tiaras perched high on the hair. The working classes had much

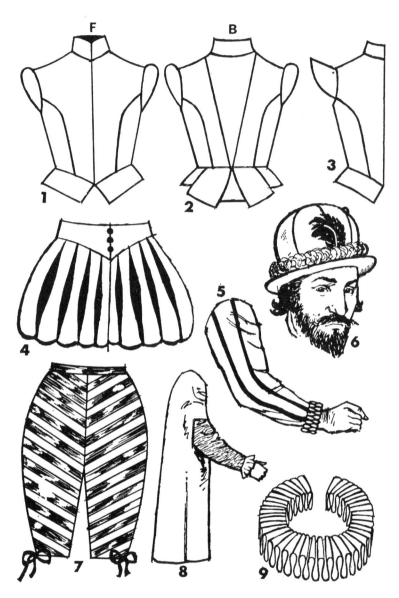

Fig. 16. ELIZABETHAN: 1 and 2 Doublet with padded roll (back and front). 3 Side view of doublet with epaulette. 4 Slops, slashed breeches. 5 Braided sleeve. 6 'Bowler' hat. 7 'Venetians'. 8 Sleeve inserted into over-sleeve. 9 Ruff.

82

simpler clothes in wool with skirts trimmed with rows of braid and lace bodices, very little different from the former period.

Later in the Elizabethan period there was a gradual change in the men's clothes. The doublets were still tight-fitting with large sleeves, but turned down collars of lawn and starched muslin, with lace edgings in scollops and points, were taking the place of ruffs, also pleated collars lying flat over the shoulder, from a high neck. Cuffs to match were turned back up on to the sleeve.

Slops altered their appearance and were called 'Trunk Hose'. They were longer and gathered top and bottom, without the slashings and strappings as heretofore.

Capes in varying lengths were still fashionable, trimmed with braids and embroidery, and in some cases lace was appliqued around the edges. Worn in a variety of ways—caught at the neck over the shoulders; over one shoulder and often carried on one arm, etc.

The hats were high crowned narrowing towards the top, in velvets and hard-blocked felts, trimmed feather, ornaments and rosettes of ribbons.

Heels were appearing on shoes which were still trimmed with ornaments and rosettes.

At this time the women's clothes were changing gradually. The waist became higher, shoulders were more rounded and sloped. Sleeves, for the most part, were melon-shaped, gathered or tucked at the wrist, with turned-back cuffs of lawn, cambric, silk and lace. There was also a three-quarter length sleeve, finishing just below the elbow, which was melon shaped and ended with a deep cuff. Bertha and cape collars—deep cut—over the shoulders, trimmed with vandyck, or scolloped edged lace. Many bows adorned the front of bodices and sleeves. Although skirts were not now stiffened, there were plenty of gathers and cartridge pleats at the waist to give masses of fullness. Sometimes there was an over-skirt open in the front, draped away to the hips, caught with bows and ornaments, and showing the under-skirt. Several petticoats were worn to give added bulk. There were short capes trimmed with lace or fur, and small velvet capes with attached hoods, having long ends of self material tying under the chin.

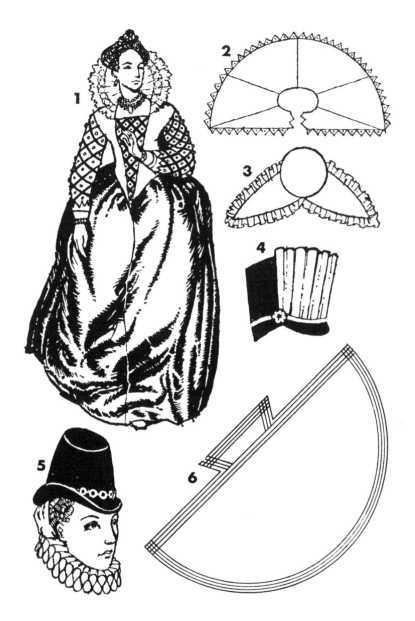

Fig. 17. ELIZABETHAN: 1 Gown. 2 and 3 Two types of collars. 4 and 5 Two types of hats. 6 Braided cape.

Large brimmed hats, with conical or flat topped crowns, feather trimmed or with rolls and drapes of self or contrasting materials twisted around the crown.

Small lace caps, or those of cambric, lawn, muslin and silk trimmed lace.

Stockings were being made of fine jersey and silk. Shoes were more pointed and with higher heels made of cork.

Figure Eight Neck Ruff and Cuffs

Materials required:—

$\frac{3}{4}$ yard of $1\frac{1}{2}''$ width white skirt petersham.

Stiff muslin, organdi, organza or starched cambric.

Cut petersham to neck size required allowing 1″ each side for overlapping. Cut a strip of material 3 yards long by 4″ wide. Make $\frac{1}{2}''$ seam in the length, turn through and press. Pleat the strip in concertina fashion to the depth required, then using two threaded needles catch top and bottom corners (like in threading beads). Make sufficient of these pleats to fit the neckband and fasten off. Mark the piece of petersham every $\frac{1}{4}''$ across the width then place each pleat on each pencil mark, catching each corner, top and bottom.

On the outer edge stitch the pleats together to form the figure eight.

Sew hooks top and bottom on overlapping piece at back of neck for fastening.

Another material which can be used exactly as it is bought is crinoline straw.

The neckband and depth of pleats can be adapted to the sizes required.

The cuffs are made in the same manner to the required wrist size, with shallow pleats.

Suitable materials for use in this period. As Tudor, but add felt.

Restoration Period

Men's clothes were now entirely different. Doublets had disappeared and knee-length jackets now made their appearance. These were slim-fitting in front and not meeting in order to show the fancy knee-length waistcoat underneath. The backs of the jackets were flat pleated in the centre back and side seams, from waist to hem, but later on these pleats were cut flared instead of flat, which gave a lot more fullness to the skirt of the jacket. Trimmed with braiding, buttons and button holes, with large pocket flaps placed low about the level of the thigh. The jackets, 'Squarecuts', were made in velvet and brocades. Sleeves were cut sleek at the head and wide at the wrist, with large turned back cuffs, these being decorated with braids, buttons and buttonholes.

Under the jackets and waistcoats were full-sleeved shirts with lace cuffs which showed below the sleeves of the jackets.

Lace and muslin cravets and stocks were worn at the neck. Waistcoats were either of plain materials with floral embroideries, or of velvet and brocade.

Knee breeches were in either self or contrasting materials. Another style of breeches were worn wide at the knees, finished with frills, or cut longer than necessary, the extra length being caught up on to the breeches with buttons.

There were large collarless overcoats with turned back revers, 'Brandenburgs', braided and buttoned, the sleeves of which were large with wide turned back cuffs, also braided and buttoned.

Silk hose was worn with high heeled shoes (some of which were red) trimmed with bows and buckles. High boots were worn with turned back cuffs, another design being a jackboot which was side-buttoned and had a fluted upstanding cuff.

Full bottomed wigs of all lengths and colours were in fashion, some with little curls over the shoulder. Short bobbed wigs and an extremely exaggerated wig called a 'Macaroni' which was

Fig. 18. RESTORATION: 1 Puritan. 2 and 8 Plumed hats. 3 'Squarecut'. 4 Jackboot. 5 'Cavalier'. 6 Shoe with red heel. 7 Breeches with turned back cuff.

wired to stand high. This latter was affected by the fops of the period. Hats were of all descriptions. Large, small, high, flat, trimmed with ostrich feather tips and bows of ribbon. A specially large hat with upswept brim, trimmed with ostrich feather plumes was worn by the cavaliers, who also wore sashes across the chest from right shoulder to left hip where it was attached to a sword.

There were gauntlet gloves with embroideries and ruched ribbon work.

Ladies' dresses were becoming more daring. The decolletage was very wide and low, revealing the cleavage of the bust. Bodices were cut low waisted, shoulders sloped, and some of the bodices were cut to a 'V' line to the waist, inserted into which were embroidered and beribboned stomachers. Neck-lines were severely plain with a draping or frilled edge softening the outline.

Skirts were full with bands of ruching and frills placed around the hips and hem. Another type was open at the front with ruchings or bands of tucking placed on the edge of the opening, which parted to reveal a pleated under-skirt, trimmed with insertions of lace and ribbons, or a quilted petticoat.

Hairstyles were upswept topped by Spanish-style head-dresses in wired lace 'Fontanges'. Another style was bunches of small curls worn each side of the head, or longer ones over the shoulders.

Large hats adorned with plumes and ribbons similar to the men, were worn.

Wool and silk stockings in bright colours were fashionable. The shoes were pointed and embroidered with high cuban or louis heels, sometimes in red.

Elbow length gloves made their appearance.

During this period there were the PURITANS who wore very sombre clothes, the men mostly in black and dark grey. The women favoured black, navy-blue and dark colours. Both sexes wore large collars and cuffs in plain white starched cambric or linen, Quaker fashion. The women had starched muslin or linen bonnets and large white aprons.

The headgear of the men was a high-crowned flat brimmed black hat.

Fig. 19. RESTORATION: 1 Gown worn with 'Fontage' head-dress. 2 Decolletage. 3 Puritan lady. 4 Quilted petticoat. 5 'Macaroni' hairstyle. 6 and 7 Two stomachers.

The Puritan children were dressed in exactly the same manner as their parents.

Suitable materials for use in this period. As Elizabethan, but add lace edgings.

Georgian and Regency Periods

Men's jackets were changing. The fullness at the back disappeared, and the skirts of the jackets were cut away in front to form a double tail at the back, where it was divided by a slit or pleat in the centre. Pockets were concealed in these openings.

The front of the jacket was either single breasted, or crossed over to a double breasted effect showing two rows of buttons, lapels were both wide and narrow, having either a 'V' cut where the stand-up collar joined the lapel, or an 'M' cut at the same place. Collars were flat at the back, and another was a double-stand collar in velvet to tone or contrast with the material of the jacket. Later the Regency jackets were completely cut away horizontally across the front at the waist and a striped or moire waistcoat was shown peeping below this line. Sleeves were narrow and fitted, with opening at the back seam showing buttons and buttonholes, or worn with a narrow cuff. There were also sleeves with full heads. Knee breeches were for the most part worn in the same materials as the jackets, or in contrasting colours, and very often in white.

'Pantaloons' were coming into favour. These were tight leg-fitting trousers, finishing at the ankle, with buttons and buttonholes, or sometimes an unadorned slit. As the pantaloons were worn very tight fitting, straps of self material or elastic were sewn to the bottoms to go under the shoes, thus preventing wrinkling. The fly front at the top of the trouser was concealed by a small flap which opened at the side forming a small covering panel. This was buttoned on either side and in the centre front.

Knickerbockers were also worn, cut loose and baggy, caught into 1″ band below the knee and buckled. They were longer than necessary to enable them to pouch when the buckle was fastened.

This form of leg-wear was comfortable and worn for all kinds of sport.

Shirts had high up-standing pointed collars over which were cravats and stocks, the two points of the collar showing above.

The cravats were of frilled lace and finished with a bow. Stocks were a long piece of silk or muslin, tying around the neck and finishing with a bow at the front or back as to the wearer's taste.

There were many varieties of overcoats, differing in lengths. Some were fitted at the waist, having broad lapels and high collars of fur or velvet, others were straight with a series of three capes on the shoulders, one above the other.

The sleeves under the capes were plain but those on the fitted coats were full headed or cape sleeves.

Top hats of all shapes and sizes were the chief headgear. There was also a flat semicircular cocked hat worn at the top of the head with points facing back and front, these latter being mostly worn at court by the nobility. Silk hose in white and pale colours was worn with the knee breeches, and a shorter type under the pantaloons. High boots, flat heeled and buckled shoes with gaiters. The hair was not worn very long when shown. Periwigs and tie powdered wigs, finishing with a curl and bow at the nape of the neck were in favour.

The men were mostly clean-shaven, but in some cases the side burns were trained to grow rather low on the face. Ornamental fobs were hung from trousers or waistcoat pockets and jewelled tiepins worn in stocks at the neck. The men's clothes of this era were greatly influenced by Beau Brummel, a dandy and a leader of men's fashion.

The women's bodices were figure-hugging and waisted, necks were cut deep with fichus and chiffon drapes worn around them. A gathered frill was worn high and tight around the neck similar to a choker necklace of today. The elbow length sleeves had frills and flares hanging from them.

Skirts were very full at the sides supported by side pads and oblong shaped hooped under-skirts.

Differing styles were double and triple tiered skirts of contrasting colours, in the former the top tier was draped at intervals, all round, and fixed with bows, the lower tier left to hang to the ankles, but in the latter style both top tiers were draped and fixed in a similar manner, leaving the third skirt plain to the ankles.

These extreme styles later gave way to more simple skirts,

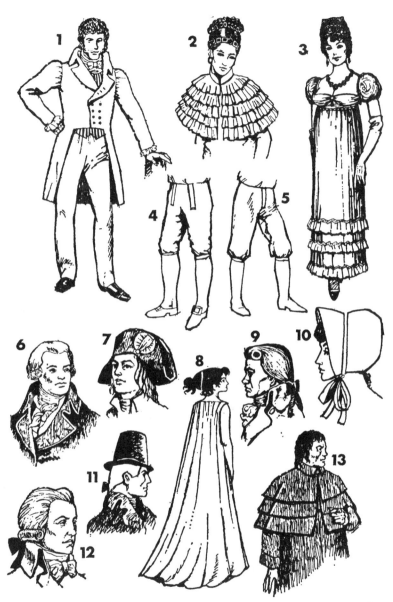

Fig. 20. REGENCY: 1 Regency man. 2 Pelerine. 3 'Directoire' style. 4 and 5 Two types of knee breeches. 6 'M' collar and revers. 7 'Cocked' hat. 8 'Watteau' back. 9 and 12 Powdered wigs. 10 Poke bonnet. 11 'Beau Brummel' hat. 13 Three-tiered caped overcoat.

with fullness evenly distributed around the sides and back of the waist.

Another feature at this time was a loose panel at the back of the gown, gathered or draped from the back of the neck and shoulders, hanging to the floor with a slight train, referred to as a 'Watteau' or a 'Sack' back.

There was also at this time a gown referred to as the 'Polonaise', which had a tight-fitting bodice and sleeves of striped material, with a double skirt, the top skirt being of the same striped material as the bodice and draped up to the back revealing a plain under-skirt. The neck and sleeves were finished with a frill of lace or muslin.

Further on in the period gowns became sleeker, but some fullness still remained in the skirt. Waists were pushed up high under the bust, the 'Empire' line or 'Directoire' style. The bodice of the gowns for daytime wear was well fitted over the bust, high necked and long sleeved. With these was worn a 'Pelerine', a cape in varying styles and proportions, either square or semicircular, frilled around the edge, or with tiered frills one upon the other. There were tiny waisted jackets with full-headed long sleeves. These jackets were also worn sleeveless. The evening dresses had low cut exposing neck-lines, the bodices being draped in the centre front cupping the bust. The skirts were ankle length and finished at the hem with frills and ruching, often in layers. There were over-skirts, short at the front and dipping at the back with embroidered bands at the edges, and some lace applique edgings. The bodice sleeves were short and puffed, or in some cases flared.

Stoles were in fashion. For the evening in transparent chiffons and silks and for the daytime in woollens. Hair was worn high, swept back with curls piled on top of the head.

Small garlands of flowers or ruchings were worn on the hair, or small ostrich feather tips or ornaments.

The headgear consisted of poke bonnets or small hard felt hats in similar shape to the men's, trimmed with ostrich feather tips and straight feather quills.

Veils, scarves and ribbons were worn over the hats and tied under the chin.

Stockings were flesh coloured and white.

Shoes were flat without heels.

Muffs were fashionable, made in velvet or cloth edged with fur, worn with a poke bonnet also edged with fur. Muffs were also made entirely in fur..

Stripes in every width were used for clothing and trimmings for both men and women. Also in furnishing and window drapes. Hence the name 'Regency Stripes'.

Suitable materials for use in this period. Taffeta, plain, striped and check, brocades, chintz, silk in small floral designs, sprigged muslin, facecloth, velour, velvet, moire, wool, jersey, cambric pique, lace, furcloth, fur, wild silk, chiffon, organza with metal thread.

Victorian Period

Men's clothes changed a great deal during this period. Colours were more sombre, brown, grey, navy, bottle green, maroon and black predominating.

Jackets were knee length trimmed with velvet collars, cuffs and pocket flaps. Shoulders were padded, and frock coats, cut away in front was a much favoured fashion. Another jacket was thigh length, cut with a fullish skirt, having pleats in the centre back and rounded at the front, the particular feature being the bold lapel and collar. Sleeves were full headed, gathered and pleated. Waistcoats were varied. Plain silk of contrasting colour to the jacket, or more elaborate of brocade and embroidery. The shapes of the waistcoats also differed. Some had small revers or roll collars, were double breasted and cut in a straight line across the waist. Others were single breasted, collarless, but had small points at the waist hanging down on to the trousers. Trousers were cut to fit tightly to the leg and in most cases were of the same material as the jacket, making a complete suit, but others were of contrasting materials and colours, often with a stripe or braid sewn at the side seam. Another fashion was the wearing of plaid tweeds and small check weaves worn with a plain jacket, the waistcoat here being of the same material as the trousers. Shirts had high collars and rows of frills down the fronts. Stocks and tied cravats were worn, the latter being a wide tie finishing with a flat bow in the front, not the fussy lace cravat of the last period. Other neckwear was a long narrow scarf wound around the neck, folded and caught in front with a pin, showing no shirt collar, worn with a collarless shirt.

There was outerwear of every description. Capes with velvet collars, coats with cape sleeves, and a new feature of the century was a raglan coat, this last being either a double breasted or fly-fronted single breasted.

A fly front is an overlap under which the buttonholes are concealed. The special thing about the raglan coat was the cut of the

Fig. 21. VICTORIAN: 1 Morning wear. 2 Evening wear. 3 'Raglan' coat. 4 and 5 Two types of waistcoats. 6 Sports jacket and cap. 7 Frilled shirt. 8 Blazer and cap.

sleeve at the shoulder. There was no armhole, the sleeve sloping into the collar seam, back and front, This style was also made in rainproof materials. For evening wear there were black cloaks with coloured satin linings. These had ornamental neck fastenings. Plain coloured, also striped stockings were in vogue, with laced up shoes. For evening there were pumps with flat bows.

Hair was long and side burns were trained to the bottom of the face, leaving the chin free. Moustaches were also worn. Top hats were the general rule.

Towards the end of the Victorian era tweeds were becoming fashionable for business and day suits, striped blazers and caps to match were worn by sportsmen and bowler hats and straw boaters made their appearance.

Evening dress and dinner jackets had lapels faced with velvet, satin or corded silk, shirt fronts were either tucked or pleated, wing collars and white bows were worn for formal occasions.

In the early Victorian era the women were wearing hooped under-skirts and crinolines, which at first were not too large, but as the era proceeded the crinoline became bigger. Bodices were fitted and pointed at the waist. Necks were high. There were cape collars adorned with frills and bands of shirring.

Some bodices were cut low to the waist in front, with tucked and pleated vests inserted.

Sleeves were very full and caught in at the wrist, or left to hang loose, dipping towards the back.

The bodices of evening gowns were cut low at the neck and exposed the shoulders, with drapings which began and ended at the centre front, extending over the shoulders around the back.

There were large bertha collars of lace trimmed small flowers and bows of coloured ribbons.

The varied skirts were frilled, tiered, flounced at the bottom with fine pleating. Double skirts, the top one being hitched up in places with flowers and bows of ribbon. Another was open in front showing an under-skirt trimmed with bands of ruchings.

Materials used were wools, bright silks, gay printed cottons, figured muslins.

Dresses were made in tartans, the skirts being tiered and edged with plain colours.

Outer garments were short mantles cut with uneven skirts dipping to the back, trimmed with rows of braid or embroidery, or fur. The sleeves were full or cape. Short fitted silk jackets had edgings of lace applique, ruchings, fringe and jet embroideries. Another decoration was in flat soutache braid.

These garments were called 'Paletot', 'Pelerine' and 'Dolman'.

Fringed paisley shawls were in fashion at this time.

Hair was severely drawn back and looped over the ears, or worn as a bun on the nape of the neck, or plaited into braids wound around the head.

The young girls wore their hair much softer in curls. For the head, bonnets were mostly in favour. There were small flat hats on top of the head and tied under the chin. Feathers, flowers and veiling adorned the headwear. Small garlands of flowers with hanging ribbon streamers were worn in the evening.

Elbow gloves were in vogue and fans were carried, as well as posies of flowers.

Under the dresses were many petticoats in cotton and taffeta, frilled with lace, and under the petticoats, long pantalette knickers, also frilled.

Shoes and boots now had small heels, and satin shoes were worn with evening clothes.

At the end of the Victorian era crinolines gave way to the bustle, which was an under-skirt with a wire cage attached to the back, over which was a double skirt, the top one aproned in front and draped up to the back, finishing with a huge bow and ends which hung to the hem. The neck-lines were low, trimmed with bands of ruchings which were repeated around the apron on the skirt. A great many artificial flowers were used. Sprays were placed at neck-lines and waists, or on the hips and in several places around the skirts, in sprays and trailing down towards the hem-line.

There were full headed and puff sleeves.

100

Fig. 22. VICTORIAN: 1 Day gown. 2 Fringed and beaded cape. 3 and 4 Two bonnets. 5 Pantalettes. 6 Evening gown. 7 Bertha collar.

Suitable materials for use in this period. Check and striped taffeta, tartan silks, satins and wools, gingham plain and check, foulard, velvet, organdi, plain and sprigged, lace, covert coating, facecloth, velour, frieze, afghalaine, woollen crepe, furcloth, fur, ermine tails for trimming, felt, corded silks and velvets, wild silks, brocade, paisley designs in wool and silk.

Edwardian Period

Men's clothes for town wear were mostly black jackets worn with striped trousers fitting tightly to the leg. There were grey waistcoats, plain or bound with braid, or in small checks, the styles being either double breasted and cut straight across at the waist, or single breasted with small points at the waist. There were brocaded waistcoats, the material being in floral and paisley designs. All waistcoats had small lapels.

A more casual town wear was a check tweed suit. Some jackets were braided around the edges, sleeve cuffs and pockets.

At this time there was a popular jacket, 'The Norfolk'. This had straps of self material from shoulder to hem, back and front with a belt, also of self material, slotted through these straps at the waist-line. A variation on this style was cut with a yoke' which is a piece of material cut in line with the shoulder but four or five inches lower, across the chest and back. The straps are placed from under this yoke to the hem of the jacket. Trousers were cut full at the waist and tight at the legs, 'Peg Top'.

Knee breeches were worn for sportswear and bicycling. With the breeches were worn long woollen socks.

Woollen cardigans and long-sleeved pullovers became a fashion, but were only worn with tweeds.

Overcoats varied in length from knee to mid-calf. Those for the winter were of heavy dark woollen materials, and occasionally gay plaids were seen, the latter being mainly worn for travelling.

There were lighter weight coats made in covert coating having velvet collars. For evening there were coats with cape sleeves, or black capes with red linings.

Top hats were still in fashion. There were also felt hats, square crowned bowlers and fedoras, straw boaters and panamas.

Men wore their hair cut short, parted in the centre. There were moustaches and beards to be seen, but mostly the men preferred to be clean shaven.

The shirt collars were either stiff, double and cut away in front,

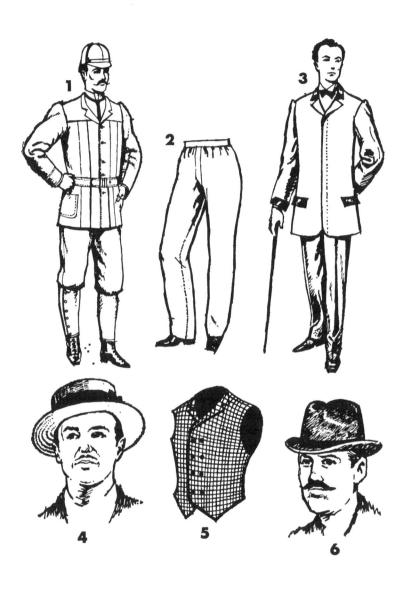

Fig. 23. EDWARDIAN: 1 Norfolk jacket, suit and cap. 2 'Pegtop' trousers. 3 Covert country overcoat. 4 Boater. 5 Check waistcoat. 6 Fedora (trilby hat).

and worn with a silk or knitted wide tie, or high-winged collars with ties and bows being worn over them. There were buttoned boots, shoes and spats.

Socks were plain, (some with coloured clocks at the sides), fancy, with spots, checks or stripes.

Cuff links were worn at the wrists, and canes and umbrellas were carried.

Edwardian ladies. The bustle cage was discarded and a back pad substituted, which after a time also disappeared. Bodices fitted to the figure, the sleeves of which were full headed and long 'Leg of Mutton'. Necks were mainly high, some bodices had the low 'V' cut to the waist with front vests and collars of lace, the collars being boned or wired, so as not to wrinkle. The inserted fronts were also in lawn, pleated and tucked, trimmed down the centre with small buttons.

The blouses, 'Shirtwaisters', were of tucked muslin and lace, or printed silks with floral designs.

The bustle, cage and pad having disappeared, the skirt was now cut flat in front, with the fullness of gathers or unpressed pleats at the back, thus giving the fashionable silhouette.

Tailor-made costumes were in fashion, with fitted and hip length jackets, with leg of mutton sleeves. The hems of the skirts were braided, either in straight rows, or in a circular design. On the wrong side of the hem a braid with a fringed edge was sewn, the purpose being to keep the hem clean, as the skirts were touching the floor. Another style of the costume jacket was cut away in the front to a round line and dipping slightly at the back. Dressy shirtwaisters were seen under these jackets. Evening dresses were very fussy, having appliques of lace and pleated frills and flounces decorating the bodices and skirts. The silhouette for evening was maintained by the wearing of a fitted and boned corset to give a wasp waist. Evening dress sleeves were either very large puffs or drapes having sleeve bustles or wire cages to support them. The petticoats under evening dresses were made of taffeta and had ruffles at the hem which added bulk at the bottom and swished as the ladies moved.

Another style of evening bodice was in chiffon draped or

105

Fig 24. EDWARDIAN: 1 Fitted bodice with leg of mutton sleeves. 2 and 7 Shirtwaister styles. 3, 8 and 9 Headgear of the time. 4 Wire cage for support of sleeve bustle. 5 Wire cage covered in material. 6 Evening dress bodice showing shirred effect. 10 One shoe style. 11 A skirt of the period. 12 Cycling bloomers. 13 Draped skirt of evening dress. 14 Back pad.

106

shirred across the bust, giving a cross-over effect. Artificial roses were in great favour and adorned most evening gowns.

Outer garments were cut full and long in order to cover the whole of the gown. The sleeves of the coats were also very large.

There were straight coats, 'Saque', having full sleeves, broad revers, collars and cuffs of velvet.

There was a variety of capes, full length and voluminous to cover the whole of the underneath, shoulder capes in fur, and in velvet trimmed fur. Stoles were also worn. Bloomers, similar to the knickerbockers of the men, but much fuller at waist and knees, pouching into woollen stockings were worn for cycling.

With these knickerbockers plain shirts with high collars and ties were worn, flat straw boaters and strong flat shoes.

Hair was high at the front, with curls on top of the head, framing the face, but at the back the hair was drawn tightly into a chignon.

The hats were cartwheel shape with masses of feathers, artificial flowers and fruit. Draped and floral toques, and rather severe flat straw hats worn with veils, caught under the chin.

Shoes were pointed with high heels, in soft kid and patent leather. Little boots with gaiter tops, buttoned at the side.

Shoes for evening were in satins and brocades. The stockings were in dark colours in silk and lisle, some having clocks, or insertions of lace.

Suitable materials for use in this period. Velour, facecloth, tweed, white flannel, striped blazer flannel, covert coating, cavalry twill, small check wools, chiffon, lace and lace edgings, worsted suitings, plain and striped, foulard, muslin, lawn, georgette, organdi, organza, felt, surah silk, satin, furcloth, fur, and marabout, taffeta.

The First World War, 1914-1918

Men's suits were becoming more like the present day wear. Waistcoats, or vests (as they were then called) were made in the same material making a three-piece suit. Jackets were cut with longer lapels, buttoning at the waist instead of at the chest as before. Trousers were wider at the bottom, with turn-up cuffs.

City gentlemen were getting away from the black jacket and striped trousers and wearing suits in navy, brown and grey, or similar materials having chalk white stripes.

Palm beach suiting made its appearance, but this was worn mainly by men who travelled abroad.

Men in offices and stores wore alpaca jackets.

The term for the men's formal wear was 'Lounge suit'.

White shirts with detachable stiff collars were the usual wear, but checked and striped shirts with collars attached were becoming fashionable.

The ties were striped, spotted or checked, cut wide, which formed a bulky knot when tied under the collar.

Overcoats were in heavy dark woollens, with broad lapels and collars which could be turned up and buttoned in inclement weather, 'Storm Collars'. There were belted overcoats, and some made in lighter colour, such as Camel cloth. Raglan cut coats were very popular, and raincoats and mackintoshes were worn. Trilby hats were of felt and tweed, straw boaters and flat caps 'Ratcatchers' were worn for sport.

Workmen were clothed in rougher woollens and tweed jackets, sleeveless leather jerkins, corduroy trousers tied with a cord under the knee, shirts with no collars, but mufflers and coloured handkerchiefs were tied around the neck. The main headwear was a cap.

Leather shoes in black and brown were the general wear, but spats in grey and beige were worn by smarter men. The working men wore boots.

Socks were plain or with checks, spots, horizontal and vertical stripes. Silk socks were commencing to become a fashion.

108

Fig. 25. 1914–18: 1 Lounge suit. 2 Afternoon gown with bishop sleeves.
3 Workman. 4 Motoring hat. 5 'Cocoon' coat. 6 'Tango' draped skirt.
7 'Pillbox' with Bird of Paradise. 7 'Pegtop' hobble skirt.

109

The women at this time wore ankle length dresses with long sleeves. Bodices were cut to the normal waist-line, but in some cases another line was cut above, under the bust to give a tight mid-riff effect, and by gathering or darting the rest of the material into this line, it gave a shape to the bust.

Sleeves were long and plain, the heads of the sleeves just set into the armholes with no fullness. Other sleeves were cut full at the wrist, gathering into a band to fit the wrist, 'Bishop'. A variation of this was cut full to the elbow, gathered into a fitted cuff from elbow to the wrist, fastened with tiny buttons and loops at the back.

There were tailored costume jackets fitting at the waist, but with varying lengths, from just below the waist down to the hips and to the knees. Cut either straight at the hem, or shaped and cut away at the front to a dipping line at the back. The fastenings were either a linked button at the waist, or buttoned entirely down the front. These jackets had long plain tailored sleeves, and skirts which were sleek. Skirts, 'Pegtop', had a draped or pleated effect at the waist. The jacket worn over this skirt had either a peplum or basque added from the waist to enable the jacket to rest over the bulky line of the skirt at the hip. Jackets were also cut in princess lines, this being in panels fitting over the bust and waist and then flaring over the hips.

Under the costumes were blouses of different designs, made in silk, muslin and lace, very fussy at the neck, having frills, cravats or long ends tied into bows under the chin. The sleeves were similar to those in men's shirts having little fullness, gathered into a wrist-band, with buttons and buttonholes, or jewelled links.

The buttons used to trim these blouses were pearl, not the flat type used on shirts, but a ball type similar to pearl beads.

The skirts of the dresses were cut in pegtop lines, some crossing over at the waist, and left open revealing the leg in movement, the 'Tango' skirt.

Peplums, and flounces with bands of velvet or fur were much worn. A particular bell-shaped peplum was stiffened at the edge and reached the knees, looking almost like a lampshade.

There were belts, and sashes cut on the cross, draped and knotted, with long ends hanging past the knees.

Lace was worn for evening dresses over silk and satin under-slips of contrasting colours—black over scarlet, brown over gold, blue over pink, etc.

Beaded trimmings and fringes were used to embellish these gowns, on hems or bands around the knees, or in vertical panels from neck and shoulders to hems.

Evening dresses were for the most part sleeveless but some had small cape sleeves edged with beaded fringe.

Coats were either cut princess line, flared at the hem, or loose at the shoulders, and narrowing into the hem, 'Cocoon', having large fur collars and cuffs. These coats were also edged in fur or had fur only at the hem-line.

Furs used were moleskin, squirrel (in grey and dyed brown), opossum and fox.

Opera cloaks were in velvet with fur trimmings.

Hair styles were upswept with bunches of curls on top, and with false hair added.

For the evening the hair was adorned with bands of beading, ospreys and birds of paradise.

Small pill-box hats with the whole bird sweeping from it, or large flat sailor hats trimmed either with pheasants feathers, or ostrich plumes. Toques of flowers and draped chiffons.

Large hats had sweeping turned-up brims trimmed with bunches of osprey.

Shoes were pointed and high-heeled, and there were high laced boots.

Silk stockings in dark colours were favoured except for evening wear, at which time they were mostly flesh coloured, when they were worn with black or white satin shoes or those dyed and beaded to match the gown. Lace and frilled chiffon parasols were carried.

Suitable materials for use in this period. As Edwardian. Add camel cloth, palmbeach suiting, corduroy, leather, chalk stripe worsteds, jersey and alpaca.

Fig. 26. TWENTIES: Sports jacket with Oxford Bags. 2 'Little Nellie Kelly' dance dress. 3 Bandeau. 4 Cloche hat. 5 Double-breasted evening jacket. 6 Day dress. 7 'Handkerchief' skirt. 8 Beaded and fringed robe.

The Twenties

The suits for men were similar to those of the previous era, but trousers became very wide at the bottoms, 'Oxford Bags'. Studying the periodicals of the time, one sees that they were also full at the waist, so that when worn under a jacket little pleats appeared where the jacket ended, but when worn with a pullover—which was often the case—the pleating did not occur.

Plus-four tweed suits were worn with fair-isle pullovers and socks mainly by golfers, but these suits were worn quite a lot otherwise.

Plus-fours are breeches full to below the knee, caught into a band and pouched.

Double breasted dinner suits were now in fashion having broad revers of corded silk. There were also single breasted suits which were now considered old fashioned.

Full evening dress was always the mode for opera and theatre first nights. These gala nights were something to be seen, the ladies in their furs and tiaras, the men in full evening dress, opera hats and cloaks.

Striped blazers with bows, or ties matching were worn with oxford bags for sporting occasions. The fashionable straw boaters also had matching hatbands.

Trilby hats and bowlers were the main headwear.

There were two-coloured shoes—black and white, or brown and white 'Correspondent', suede shoes were being seen.

Socks were of vivid checks and stripes.

At the beginning of the twenties the skirts of women's day dresses were well below the knee and evening dresses were ankle length. In the day time the sleeves were generally long.

There were tailored costumes and a special feature was a double breasted style similar to the men, with broad pointed revers fastening with four or six buttons. A new style was a two-piece suit comprising a dress and a jacket in the same material or a dress and a long coat. These coats were cut to meet at the

113

centre front, referred to as 'Edge to Edge'. Mostly collarless, having bands of tucking or corded work in a floral design, 'Italian Quilting', down both edges. Another feature of the two-piece was the front panel of the dress being appliqued in a design of leaves and flowers on net, this being repeated on the edges of the coat, and bottoms of sleeves.

These garments were made in either wool, or silk marocain, the latter being a heavy crinkly material, now extinct. Evening dresses were in lace and faconné, mostly sleeveless with boat-shaped necks and the low waists were at hip level. There was a popular style 'Little Nellie Kelly' named after a musical show in which June, a very lovely star appeared wearing the dress. The bodice was simple and sleeveless, with a boat neck, the skirt being slit in front from the low waist showing an under-skirt of over-lapping $1\frac{1}{2}''$ frills. This gown was surely copied by every bride, bridesmaid and ballroom dancer at that time. Later on in the twenties the dresses became shorter—just showing the knee. Evening gowns had uneven dipping hemlines.

The bodices had simple neck-lines, 'V', round or boat shaped. A boat neck is a long high line from shoulder to shoulder with the shoulder seam being about 2″ wide.

Sleeves were small and plain, set into a normal armhole. The newer skirts for day wear were pleated either in tiny accordian pleats, or 2″ box pleats, which fell from the low waist-line, which was always at hip length. There were belts and sashes with long ends, hanging to the hem, fixed at this waist-line.

The skirts of the new evening gowns—which finished at the knee—had bands of fox fur trimming around the hem, or as an alternative bands of marabout, which is an ostrich feather trimming clipped to look like fur. It is made in several widths, from a single strand of 1″ onwards. Another trimming in this manner were ruchings of taffeta, cut on the cross, gathered and frayed at the edge.

Different evening skirts and uneven hemlines dipping from knee to ankles, from front to back, or with two dropping side panels.

'Handkerchief' skirts consisted of square pieces of georgette or

114

chiffon, with one corner caught at the waist-line all round, and hanging in points to the hem. The bodices of evening dresses were straight and simple, sleeveless, having boat necks or cut in a straight line, just at the top of the bust, supported by narrow shoulder straps, 'Camisole Line'. There were lace dresses worn over contrasting coloured camisole slips, also beaded robes made of net or lace, covered in beads in floral and leafy designs, having beaded fringe at the hem. These were open at the sides, up to the waist-line, from which hung flares of chiffon or georgette. Artificial flowers, also large bushy feather flowers, were worn at shoulders and waistlines.

Loose coats of wool and velvet with fox trimmings were worn for day and evening.

A garment called an opera cloak was very popular for evening wear, made in velvet or brocade, lined with contrasting satin, the shape being a square gathered at the neck into a bolster collar, plain or gauged on to cords, padded with wadding, fastened at the neck with ties of self material. These opera cloaks could be made more glamorous by trimming with fox, or lined with flat fur.

The hair was cut short 'Bobbed', 'Shingled', and an even shorter style 'Eton crop'.

A bandeau was worn around the hair copied from the tennis star Suzanne Lenglen.

The hats were 'Cloche', or large with turned back brims, and feather trimmings at the sides. Cartwheels, in leghorns, or crinolines were of straw.

Silk stockings were always flesh coloured and worn with ankle strap and court shoes which had very pointed toes and louis heels.

Long beaded or short pearl necklaces were worn with drop earrings.

Suitable materials for use in this period. Chalk stripe flannel, barathea, covert coating, serge, blazer flannel, striped and plain, tweed, light and dark heavy coating, wool georgette, wool crepe, lace, satin backed crepe, crepe romaine, georgette, chiffon, faconné, velvet, satin, taffeta, furcloth, fur, brocade, felt, marocain, fringe in all widths, velvet and poplin.

Fig. 27. THIRTIES: 1 Godet skirt. 2 Large straw hat. 3 Evening gown with panelled skirt and circular cuffs. 4 Bias-cut evening gown. 5 'Coal-skuttle' hat. 6 Tunic blouse with monk's collar.

116

The Thirties

Men's clothes underwent little change. Single and double breasted jackets continued to be in fashion, trousers being not quite so wide at the bottoms, but still having turn-ups. Lapels on the double breasted jackets were very pointed and broad.

The city gent was wearing a black jacket, striped trousers, topped by a bowler, and always carried a rolled umbrella. Double breasted navy blazers and grey flannels were a week-end wear, white flannels were kept mainly for cricket and tennis. Belted overcoats and raincoats were in fashion, but the dark, loose, velvet-collared overcoat was still being worn by the smarter man.

Shirts had long pointed collars, ties were wide and colourful. Evening tails were still popular as well as double breasted dinner suits.

Homberg hats were being seen and the trilby hats had wider snap brims. A 'Homberg' is a felt hat with a curled brim.

Socks were still very colourful and suede shoes were now being worn a great deal.

In the thirties ladies' clothes changed completely. Skirt hems dropped to mid-calf, evening skirts being ankle length.

Bodices were pouched at the natural waist-line, neck-lines were scooped low in 'cowls' back and front, the latter being a draped effect, the material being cut on the cross and allowed to fall naturally.

Evening dresses were mainly cut on the cross or bias, which allowed them to cling to the figure, sleeves were tight and long. Another sleeve was cut tight to the elbow with a complete circular cuff hanging therefrom to the wrist.

Another fashion was tunic jumpers, being long blouses, reaching to the hips or knees, made in floral silks and satins, worn with a plain dark skirt, a sash made from the material of the jumper was tied at the waist and hung to the skirt at the hem. The jumpers were usually finished with 'monk's' collars, a wide piece of material cut on the bias, doubled, and mounted on to a deep round neckline, tied with a bow and ends at front, back, or side, wherever desired.

The sleeves were usually bishop.

Flowing dresses, with small jackets to match were made in flowered chiffons and georgettes. There were long sleeved dresses, with sleeveless jackets made in patterned silks and foulards.

A popular skirt line was fitted to the knee, flaring therefrom to the ankles, achieved by either godets insetred into the seams all round, or crossway pieces with the corners left on and attached to the skirt, in eight or ten places. Tailored suits were worn with fussy waist blouses. Woollen jumpers and cardigans were being worn a lot, the vogue was for hand-knitted garments, mostly made by the wearers themselves.

The hats were either tiny pillboxes or a type of 'Coalscuttle'. Large straw hats were worn with floral outfits for garden parties and race meetings. Shoes were either plain court or strapped across the instep.

Suitable materials for use in this period. Flowered chiffons and georgettes, slipper and duchesse satin, grosgrain, ottoman, velvet, lace, worsted tweeds, white, grey and navy flannel, barathea, tweed, woollen crepe and georgette, marocain, gaberdine.

The Forties

In the early years, during the second world war, the powers that be decided Austerity in Fashion, and coupons for clothes. There was very little change in men's lounge suits, having to make do with what they had, owing to the fact that the women were using their husbands' and boy friends' clothing coupons.

However, there was a difference in men's evening clothes, full evening wear being confined to head waiters. Dinner suits were the main evening apparel, and a new style of dinner jacket was now to be seen, this being single breasted with a shawl collar in satin or petersham.

The 'Shawl' is a roll collar in shape similar to the roll collar on dressing gowns, but narrower.

A new colour for dinner suits, 'Midnight Blue', was a very dark navy which looked excellent under electric light. Waistcoats became a thing of the past and the style was a two-piece suit, with double or single breasted jacket, the trousers worn either belted or self-supporting with buttons and concealed elastic in the waist.

Overcoats were mainly heavy and belted. Demobbed officers who had retained their military overcoats, 'British Warms', were wearing them. These were short and very smart, made in heavy wool of a light fawn colour. 'Duffle' coats, which were loose and shapeless were worn by men and women. The garments fastened across the neck and chest and had a hood attached.

It was quite amusing to see a city gentleman in his duffle coat worn over his black jacket and striped trousers, complete with a bowler hat, brief case and rolled umbrella. Shoes were sturdy and little boottees in suede and leather were coming into fashion.

The war influence on women's clothes was obvious in the military cut and padded shoulders of the suits and coats. Shoulders in dresses also had the exaggerated padded outline, with pleated sleeveheads in the manner of the leg of mutton sleeves of the Edwardian period.

Fig. 28. Forties: 1 Evening suit with 'shawl' collar. 2 'New Look' cocktail gown. 3 Day suit. 4 Day suit ('New Look'). 5 and 6 Two hats. 7 'Midriff' afternoon gown. 8 and 9 Platform and wedge shoes.

The mid-riff high-busted line was again in evidence. Skirts were shorter, suit skirts being 'knife' pleated in the back or having a wrap over pleat on one side at back or front, or both.

Evening, or 'dinner' dresses as they were then called (gala and ball gowns were non-existent) were long and had long or short sleeves, with the leg of mutton heads. At this time no decorations such as beading or embroidery were allowed.

Evening dresses were mostly made in moss crepe which was the foremost material available, as it draped and hung well. There were dinner gowns in fine wools.

Tweeds and suitings were made into simple day dresses and skirts, the latter being worn with hand-knitted matching jumpers and cardigans, 'Twin Set'. Trousers became a practical wear, sometimes with matching jackets, which were called 'Slacks' and 'Slack' suits. Top coats were plain tailored and serviceable, having no fur trimmings.

In the late forties Christian Dior came along with his 'New Look', mid-calf length skirts, cut very full, fitted short jackets with natural shoulder line. Padded shoulders were out, and the padding was removed from all existing clothes, and women were graceful again.

Existing skirts were lengthened by the adding and inserting of bands of velvet and petersham trimmed with braiding. It was easy to see which of the clothes were new and which had been altered.

These 'make do and mend' methods were necessary as coupons were still having to be given for materials.

Furnishing fabrics were free of coupons for a while and some plays were dressed entirely with these materials, but eventually the Board of Trade put even these materials on coupons.

Embroideries were again being shown in the Paris collections. The ban was lifted in England in consequence of which embroideries and fancy trimmings were again in use.

Evening dresses sparkled again. Velvets and silks reappeared, and fur was used for collars and trimmings.

Hats were worn again instead of service caps and handkerchiefs tied around the head.

Silk stockings were still the vogue, but the first 'Nylons' were beginning to appear.

Shoes became more graceful and not so serviceable as heretofore.

Suitable materials for use in this period. Barathea, tweed, woollen coatings, camel coatings, moss crepe, wool crepe, velvet, gaberdine.

The Fifties

Men's clothes went through a lot of changes. Jackets were much shorter with velvet collars appearing on some, and they were buttoned higher up on the chest. The sleeves had cuffs. This was a 'Teddy Boy' style adapted from the Edwardian period. Trousers were tighter with the turn-ups removed. The young men of the fifties altered their style of dress frequently.

A new style of jacket, looser fitting, having slits either at the back or sides, was due to an 'Italian' influence from which it was copied. These trousers were extremely tight.

Materials used were light-weight woollen mohairs and woven silk tweeds.

The blazers were double or single breasted, made in navy flannel or gaberdine worn with beige cavalry twill trousers and grey flannels.

White 'Tee' shirts and shorts were worn for tennis.

Shoes were in suede and leather, and for summer in canvas in all colours—'Bumpers' or 'Sneakers'.

Plastic mackintoshes were sold by the hundreds. These were folded small and carried everywhere.

There were shirts with horizontal stripes, these stripes appearing on ties which were worn very narrow. Also popular were narrow knitted ties.

Socks were made of nylon.

There were trilby hats made in felt and tweed, also a popular head covering was a sporting cap, block in felt (a type of beret) with a peak brim.

The New Look continued to be fashionable in the fifties. Day dresses were in fine wool and stiff silks.

Bodices were fitted buttoning either down the back or front, or zipped up the back, or at side seam. Jumper suits were very popular with full pleated skirts. Navy blue wools and silks were very fashionable, trimmed with white collars and cuffs, vests and bows of pique, and broderie anglaise.

Fig. 29. FIFTIES: 1 Italian style. 2 Back view, with vents. 3 'Sunray' skirt with 'Bolero' jacket. 4 'Kangol' cap. 5 'Sweetheart' neckline. 6 Strapless dance dress. 7 'Sloppy Joe' sweater. 8, 9 and 10 'Separates'.

Short 'bolero' jackets, finishing above the waist-line were in vogue. There were many petticoats under the skirts of both day and evening dresses to give a bouffant effect. Occasionally a hoop was worn at the hem but this proved uncomfortable and was soon dropped. Summer clothes were very gay with their full skirts and petticoats in floral silks, and cottons.

'Separates' became a vogue, even for evening wear, the latter being lace or beaded tops worn with black skirts.

The summer day skirts were in printed cottons and flounced. The flouncing was done by cutting the material into strips which are gathered one on to the other, each lower strip being twice the length of the one above. There were usually four or five tiers, the last being very full.

Plain full skirts were made in sail cloth, obtainable in all bright colours, cut either circular or with unpressed pleats at the waist, adorned with large patch pockets. A trimming on these skirts was a piping of a contrasting colour around the hem and pockets.

The tops of the separates were varied, some were sleeveless, or had small puff sleeves, or worn strapless and boned.

Evening dresses became shorter and finished about 12″ from the ground—ballet length, very full, with many petticoats, some frilled like 'Can Can' petticoats. Bodices were strapless, being supported by boning, sometimes finished at the top edge with small collars and frills. Lace was often used for evening gowns beaded, or re-embroidered with a cord picking out the design. There were cocktail dresses which had deep necks, framed with a shawl collar. The skirts were very full and the sleeves tiny.

Another style was a sleek dress in brocade with a square or 'Sweetheart' neck-line, having a fitted jacket in self material. The dresses were sleeveless and were cut low at the back, so that when the jacket was removed they could be worn as dinner dresses.

In the late fifties the 'Teenagers' wore tight slacks, with sweaters and pullovers, the slacks became tighter as the sweaters became longer and larger, referred to as 'Sloppy Joes'. This attire was worn in jazz clubs and coffee bars.

At this time the Paris collection showed some shapeless garments, 'Sack', which at first were laughed at, but eventually they became the rage and every woman wanted to wear one. This dress was cut in one piece from neck to hem very short and tight around the knees with not a belt in sight.

Day and evening dresses were now sleeker. Full skirts went out of fashion.

Loose day coats, 'Tent', were now appearing and fur collars and trimmings were worn.

Mink and fox capes and stoles in shades of brown, beige, grey and white were worn in the evening.

There were stoles matching the gowns and those in wool of contrasting colours.

Gloves and shoes made in the same material as the dress were also worn.

A particular style for daytime was a suit cut 'Magyar' fashion, being sleeves cut in one with the bodice. The skirt was very tight necessitating small slits left at either side or back seams to enable the wearer to walk.

The shoes in the early fifties had platform soles or wedge heels, but these gave way to the ankle strap and court shoes with graceful high heels.

Hats were of all shapes and sizes. Pillboxes, draped toques, flowered and feathered.

Over summer dresses short coats in pastel shades and white were to be seen.

Pleated dresses and shorts were worn for tennis.

Suitable materials for use in this period. Tweed, worsted wools, mohair, silk tweed, velvet, wool crepe, afghalaine, flannel, printed cottons, sail cloth, lace, brocade, wild silk, taffeta, poplin, grosgrain, cavalry twill, slipper and duchesse satins, pique, sharkskin, linen, chiffon.

The Sixties

Men's clothes were changing again. Turn-ups were gone from trousers which were tighter than ever, some having slits on the outside seams at the ankles. Jacket lapels were narrower, and some worn by the younger men were without lapels, but often with a small flat collar. There were corduroy velvet suits, and corduroy velvet jackets worn with worsted trousers, or vice versa. Another style of jacket was 'Battledress', short and finishing with a band at the waist.

There were leather overcoats, jackets and trousers. A popular wear with the young, were coloured cotton 'jeans', very tight, worn with woollen pullovers and cardigans. There were short 'car' coats, trimmed fur and furcloth. Leather hats and caps and the latter in coloured denims. Firstly the older men frowned on this new way of dress but gradually they began to wear the new casual styles, not carrying it to extremes as in the case of the youngsters.

In 1964 with the advent of the Beatles and other singing groups young men wore their hair long and copied the style of dress of their singing idols.

Very pointed shoes, 'Winkle Pickers', were imported from Italy, and boottees were of leather, suede and fur—'Chelsea' and 'Beatle' boots. Russian boots were being worn by both sexes.

The outline of the women of the sixties was sleek. Waist-lines in their right place. Skirts with peg-top pleats, belts were seldom worn.

Some dresses were cut from shoulder to hem in one piece. A gathered detail, or a button flap suggested the waist, or small belts inserted into the back.

Other styles were buttoned through from neck to hem, or having fly-away panels from the shoulders at the back caught into the waist, from which they were left loose. Jumper suits pouched at the hips, and there were simple boat-necked dresses with matching short jackets. The tailored suit was not seen, but

Fig. 30. SIXTIES: 1 Casual jacket. 2 'Beatle' boots. 3 'Battledress' jacket. 4 'Sinatra' straw hat. 5 'Beatle' cap. 6 Collarless 'Beatle' jacket. 7 Russian boots with 'Winkle-Picker' toecap.

its place was taken by the 'dressmaker' suit, the jackets collarless with contrasting scarves tucked into the neck. Some suits had the lining of the jackets matching the blouses, in flowered and spotted printed silks, and thin wools.

Top coats were in either wool or silk, cut straight, with large collars and having half belts or side belts at hip level.

For evening wear there were short beaded tunics, and dresses with 'Harem' skirts which were gathered on to a lining and pouched at the hem. There were short and pleated chiffon dresses worn, in many bright colours.

A skirt seen more often on the stage was tight to the knees with a full bell-shaped flounce gathered therefrom to the floor. This was a difficult skirt to walk in, but effective if the wearer stayed in one place. Leather and suede coats and suits were in fashion as well as dresses. One dress in the pinafore style was worn over jumpers and blouses in the day time, and when worn alone, served as a cocktail or dinner dress.

Leather hats and caps were similar to those of the men. Footwear was court and strapped shoes with very thin heels, 'Stilletto', and very pointed toes. Russian boots in all colours, and white.

In 1963 and '64 young 'Pop' artists appeared before the public in concert halls and on television wearing the latest styles in dresses which were trimmed frills of lace and broderie anglais at neck, sleeves and hem. These were created by up and coming young designers, and the styles were copied by teenage fans. In 1965 there was a new Parisian designer, Couregges, whose unusual styles were widely worn. Other designers were inspired to create similar clothes. These dresses were on symmetrical lines, introducing several colours into one garment.

In 1966 young people's clothes became more flamboyant than ever. Topcoats, jackets, trousers, hats and caps were made in brightly coloured american cloth—now called P.V.C. (Poly Vinyl Chloride) and were worn by both sexes.

Some young men wore tight trousers made from two or three different coloured sections of materials resembling parti-coloured tights of the medieval times, these were cut low at the waist and called 'Hipsters', worn with wide plain and striped belts. Shirts

129

Fig. 31. SIXTIES: 1 'Mandarin' dress. 2 'Fly-away' panel. 3 Dressmaker suit. 4 Topcoat. 5 Stage or TV evening dress. 6 and 7 'Jaunty' hats.

were also made in this manner. Another style of shirt was in a vivid flowered material with plain long pointed collar and plain cuff. And this same style was also seen using large checked materials instead of flowered.

Jackets were cut in a variety of ways—collarless—high Russian stand-up collars, or with narrow lapels—strapped in the Norfolk jacket way with epaulettes buttoned on the shoulder. Blazers were double breasted—high-buttoned with long slits and vents, either at the back or sides.

Ties were wider and also very flowered.

Oddly enough with all this 'Pop' gear (as it was called) black socks and shoes and boottees were mostly worn.

The girls' skirts were becoming very much shorter, finishing at from 4″ to 6″ above the knee. Sleeves were in some cases long or non-existent, leaving cut-away armholes at the tops of dresses and jumpers. The high Russian boots were still very fashionable, mostly in white leather, and they were now also being made in transparent and coloured P.V.C., the styling being cut-out over the toes and uppers trimmed with lacings and bows. Topcoats were short with fluffy wool trimmings at collars, cuffs and hems. Some had Mongolian shaggy lamb fur collars in grey, off-white or dyed to match the cloth of the coat. Lace patterned stockings were in all colours and worn with all this gear.

All the latest clothes for both sexes could be seen in shops in Carnaby Street, a narrow thoroughfare behind and running parallel with Regent Street in the west-end of London, which was always crowded with customers and sight-seers.

The Paris houses were also using P.V.C. to trim dresses and coats. Yves St. Laurent designed a white mink coat with bands of black P.V.C. across it, and this coat was seen on Margot Fonteyn.

Young girls were wearing their hair shorter in lots of cases, but the males seemed to prefer theirs long.

In the latter part of 1967 there was a phase of romanticism in the garments of the young people. They wore silk caftans with braided edges, also flowered and vivid figured three-quarter length jackets and trousers, worn with ropes of beads and

131

bells on chains. All varieties of flowers were worn or carried

The pop groups and singers on televison were mostly wearing fancy dress of some kind.

PSYCHEDELIC was the word used to describe the colours and happenings at this time.

In the late sixties, young girls' skirts were getting shorter still, as much as eight inches above the knee, and the name given to these abbreviated garments was 'Mini-skirt'. Mary Quant—a new designer—was given the credit for the appearance of these mini-skirts, but other designers in London and Paris were quick to follow suit. Dresses became so short that they resembled long blouses or jumpers being worn without skirts.

Materials used were vivid coloured wools and silks printed in floral, check and geometrical patterns in bold outlines, the name given to these designs being 'Pop Art'. Trouser suits with longish jackets and flared bell bottom trousers were popular, made in all these materials.

The girls' shoes were in vivid colours, low heeled, square-toed, and with straps across the instep (resembling childrens' styles).

The young boys began a phase of wearing old military jackets in all colours, with navy-blue or black capes over them, and some young girls could be seen wearing these capes as well.

The hair was still worn long by the young males. They also had a liking for moustaches, beards and long full sideburns, similar to those of the early Victorian era.

What of the future? Who knows? Fashion is such a fickle jade.

Suitable materials for use in this period. Tweed, wool jersey, metal thread jersey, plaid woollens, barathea, gaberdine, flannel, velvet, corduroy, leather, suede, chiffon, linen, crepe backed satin, afghalaine, organza, taffeta, wild silk, satin, pique, poplin, lace, broderie anglaise, denim, gingham, flowered and spotted silks and wools, paisley and flowered delaine.

Head Sizes (Men and Women)

Size						Inches
$5\frac{3}{4}$	..	..	..	..	..	$18\frac{1}{2}$
$5\frac{7}{8}$	..	..	..	..	..	19
6	..	..	..	..	..	$19\frac{1}{4}$
$6\frac{1}{8}$	..	..	..	..	..	$19\frac{3}{4}$
$6\frac{1}{4}$	..	..	..	..	..	$20\frac{1}{8}$
$6\frac{3}{8}$	..	..	..	..	..	$20\frac{1}{2}$
$6\frac{1}{2}$	..	..	..	..	..	$20\frac{7}{8}$
$6\frac{5}{8}$	..	..	..	..	..	$21\frac{1}{4}$
$6\frac{3}{4}$	..	..	..	..	..	$21\frac{5}{8}$
$6\frac{7}{8}$	..	..	..	..	..	$22\frac{1}{8}$
7	..	..	..	..	..	$22\frac{1}{2}$
$7\frac{1}{8}$	..	..	..	..	..	$22\frac{7}{8}$
$7\frac{1}{4}$	..	..	..	..	..	$23\frac{1}{4}$
$7\frac{3}{8}$	..	..	..	..	..	$23\frac{5}{8}$
$7\frac{1}{2}$	..	..	..	..	..	24
$7\frac{5}{8}$	..	..	..	..	..	$24\frac{3}{8}$
$7\frac{3}{4}$	..	..	..	..	..	$24\frac{3}{4}$

Millinery

Professional millinery is an art which is only acquired after an apprenticeship and years of experience. It is also taught in evening classes at L.C.C. schools. In every amateur dramatic society's workroom or wardrobe there is a gifted person who sews and it is to this person that these elementary hints will be useful.

ARTICLES AND MATERIALS NEEDED

A hat block or wig block.

A stretching block. This is a head shape divided into two halves, with a rod going through, attached to a handle, by which it is adjusted to all sizes.

A yardstick and brown paper or unbleached calico for patterns. A velvet board or velvet sleeve board the latter being much smaller and will be useful for pressing seams in velvet. Black and white millinery wire sold in rings of various widths. A medium one is the most pliable. Wire clippers and pliers.

Buckram, and felt by the yard, made in all colours. There is also a heavy quality sold in furnishing departments, mainly used for floors and display purposes. When using felt for shapes do not allow seams, but cut net and oversew all seams on the wrong side.

Millinery work is mostly done by hand, but joins and head-linings can be machined. Sometimes rows of machine stitching are a feature of the hat.

Buckram shapes in all styles can be purchased in stores and millinery suppliers. These can be covered in silks and velvets or flowers.

HOODS—not to be confused with Period hoods, but the name by which large unmade shapes of felt, velour and straw are known. (Also obtainable at the millinery suppliers). These are useful for making cavalier hats by tacking up one side and adding ostrich plumes.

They can also be made into tricornes by tacking up three sides,

134

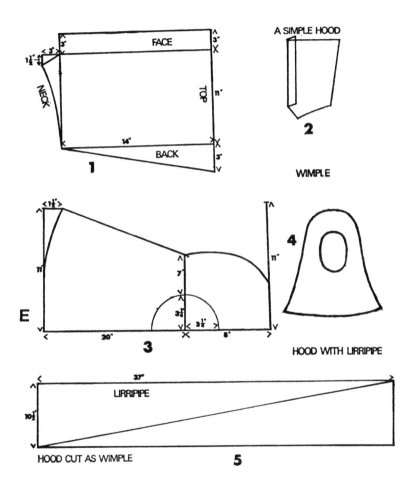

Fig. 32. 1, 2, 3, 4, and 5.

or by adding flowers, feathers, ribbons and artificial fruit can be trimmed into Edwardian gear.

In the last case the edges should be wired to support the trimmings.

Buckram shapes in top hats, etc., for men, straw sailor hats and boaters can be obtained at the theatrical material suppliers.

Small sized boaters, painted black or colours, can be trimmed with ribbons or flowers to make ladies' hats of certain periods.

Men's discarded felt hats should be retained as they can be reblocked into other styles by putting them on the block, steaming with a wet rag and hot iron. If the edges of these hats are bound with ribbon, remove it, then the shapes will become more pliable.

The following are a few simple styles which should be quite easy to make:—

It is advisable to make a pattern first, remembering to use a yardstick for all straight and diagonal lines, rounded and semcircular lines are done freehand.

A PLAIN HOOD (Fig. 32)—Take a piece of brown paper or calico and on this draw a vertical line 14″ in length. At the top and bottom of this draw two lines horizontally, of 11″ each, then another vertical line of 14″ thus forming a rectangle. From the nearest top corner add 3″ then draw a diagonal line from that point to the bottom. This is the back of the hood. At the bottom corner, furthest away, add 4½″ on to the vertical line, then mark a spot 1½″ back, then draw a line from this mark to the original corner, returning to the spot mark draw a semicircular line to the bottom back corner forming the neck.

The face opening which is the vertical line opposite to the back. If required plain, do no more, but if a turn back cuff is wanted, add 3″ at the top and bottom corners horizontally, then draw another vertical line. Cut out in all outer edges.

Fold material double then place pattern on it with the top of the hood at the fold—which is the horizontal line opposite to the neck. Cut the hood, allow seams unless making in felt.

When making a turn back cuff at the face, there must be a 6″ piece seamed at the front edge and lined to allow the right side of the material to turn back. If the hood is in felt it is unnecessary to do this.

This is just a face hood, but should a shoulder or full length cape be required it should be attached at the neck-line.

WIMPLE—To make pattern fold a piece of paper or calico, this makes the centre line. On this line measure 20″ from top to bottom making a horizontal line of 11″ at each end. Mark a spot 8″ down from top and from this spot a horizontal line of 7″. From the centre line at top draw a semicircular line to this mark, continuing with a diagonal line to the bottom outside corner. From the bottom corner place a mark $1\frac{1}{2}$″ upwards and from this mark draw a semicircular line to the bottom centre front.

For the face hole go back to the mark made 8″ down from the top. Making this the centre, mark $3\frac{1}{4}$″ above and below and outwards. Draw a semicircular line from top to bottom taking in the side. This gives a half circle. Cut out this half circle, and all outside edges. This is the front of the wimple. Repeat the process for the back omitting the face hole. Open up the pattern, place on material and cut out. Line the face hole with a piece cut in the same shape, seam all round, leaving the bottom open. Hem this. If in felt it is not necessary to line the hole, or hem. Felt does not fray.

HOOD with LIRRIPIPE—Cut front exactly as wimple with the face hole. For the back fold pattern and when cutting instead of the fold at the centre back, allow a seam. Join this seam, allowing a 5″ space at the top. Make as for the wimple.

For the lirripipe one yard long, measure a piece of material 37″ long by $10\frac{1}{2}$″ wide. Fold double lengthwise. From one corner at the bottom up to the centre at the top, draw a diagonal line. Cut in this line, but allowing seam. Stitch together leaving bottom open. Pad with cotton wool and insert the bottom into the 5″ space left on the back of the hood. If the lirripipe is required soft, no padding should be used. The length of the lirripipe can be varied by adding or subtracting on the centre line of the pattern.

A MUMMERS OR JESTERS HOOD—For pattern fold paper or calico in half, making centre line measuring 20″ long. At top a horizontal line of $9\frac{1}{2}$″, at bottom a horizontal line of 11″. From

137

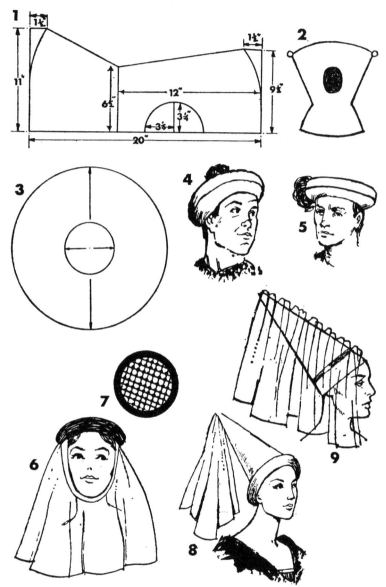

Fig. 33. 1 and 2 Jester's hood. 3 Pattern for 'Tam-O-Shanter' (4). 4 'Tam-O-Shanter' (worn). 5 Bonet. 6 and 7 Top and front view of medieval headroll with barbette and veiling. 8 and 9 Hennin, two ways of draping veiling.

138

top outside corner mark $1\frac{1}{2}''$ down and make a semicircular line from this mark to the centre front. At bottom outside corner mark $1\frac{1}{2}''$ up, then do a semicircular line to the centre front. 12″ from the centre front put a horizontal line of $6\frac{1}{2}''$. From top outside corner make a diagonal line to this mark and continue on to the bottom corner.

For the face hole mark 8″ down from centre front, making this the centre, mark $3\frac{1}{4}''$ up, down and across, making this your guide draw a semicircle, cut out in all marks. This is the front. Make another similar piece, without the face hole, for the back. Open out the pattern, and lay on the material. Cut out, line the face hole, seam all round leaving bottom open, and hem. Pad the ear corners with wadding and secure, sew a bell on each corner.

PILLBOX—(Three types). A straight one $2\frac{1}{2}''$ in depth. When cutting in buckram allow seams. In felt cut net. This applies to all shapes here mentioned.

1. Cut a straight piece 22″ long by $2\frac{1}{2}''$ wide and a circle measuring 22″ around the edge. Join the long piece together and the top edge to the circle. Wire the bottom edge by over-sewing and bind with tape. The buckram pillbox is now ready for covering with material or soft felt. When cutting material to cover brim allow $1\frac{1}{2}''$ more to turn up under and line with taffeta. When using the harder felt, make simply in the felt with no buckram or lining.

2. The narrow top shape (fez). Cut a semicircular crown 22″ at the head 16″ at the top, 5″ wide and a circle measuring 16″ around the edge. Make as No. 1.

3. Wider top shape. Cut a semicircular piece, 22″ at head, 28″ at top, $2\frac{1}{2}''$ wide and a circle of 28″ around the edge. Make as No. 1.

These shapes are for 22″ head fittings equalling $6\frac{7}{8}$. If other sizes and depths are wanted adjustments can be made accordingly.

TAM O'SHANTER—Tammy. Cut two circles measuring 10″ across, mount on to stiff muslin (not if using felt). In one piece, make another circle in the centre measuring 6″ across, for the head. Seam the two circles together on the outer edges, press seam open on sleeve board or bust pad, adjust the opening to fit required head measurement and bind or face with material cut on the cross, or bias tape. If a stand-up brim is wanted, cut a

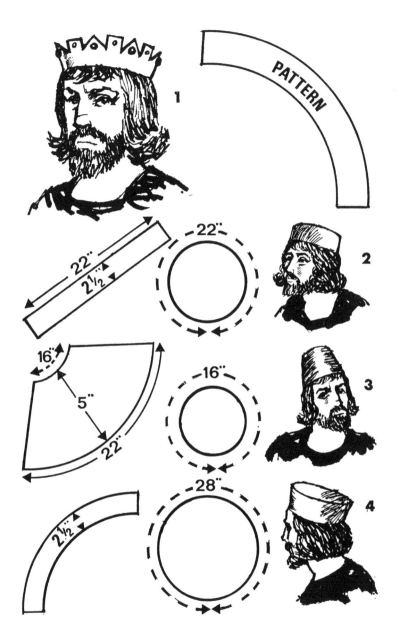

Fig. 34. 1 Crown and pattern. 2 Straight pillbox and pattern. 3 Fez pillbox and pattern. 4 Wider top pillbox and pattern.

straight piece of material to the length and double the width required, mount it on stiff muslin, join it, fold double in the length, then insert the raw edges into the head opening.

BONET (Tudor). The top is exactly as the tam-o-shanter but without the straight brim. The bottom part, which is the brim, is cut first in buckram in exactly the same sized circle as the under-part of the tammy, with an opening for the head. The outer edge is wired and bound with tape, the material is placed over and the edge tucked under. Another piece of material is sewn and turned in onto the edge. When brim is made join the brim and crown at the head opening, line with taffeta. If making in felt, a piece of buck-ram is placed between two layers of felt and oversewn at the edge.

HENNIN—(Medieval Conical Head Dress). Cut a piece of buckram 18″ long by 24″ wide. This is for a 23″ head size. Alter as necessary. Mark a centre line, top to bottom, then a diagonal line each side from outside bottom corners to the centre at top. Cut in this line, allowing a seam. Join by over-lapping. Oversew wire at bottom and bind edge with tape. Cover the shape with required material which should be seamed, not overlapped, allowing 2″ at bottom for turning up underneath. Sew a piece of 1″ gold braid around at 2″ above bottom, or make a cuff by cutting a piece of self, or contrasting material on the cross 24″ by 5″ wide, seam across and double in the length, and attach to the bottom of the shape, turning the two raw edges under, leaving the folded edge of the cuff to show. Then line with taffeta. Cut a square of chiffon or voile, or a circular flare, and attach to the point.

Another style is to attach the square of chiffon all down from top to bottom, pleating gently.

FLAT MEDIEVAL HEADROLL—This looks best in velvet, but can be made in felt or other materials. Cut on the cross a length, 24″ by 5″ in width, for a 23″ headsize, but alter if required. Having made a roll of wadding of 2″ in circumference, cover this with the material by sewing one edge over the other, turning in the top edge. Join to make a circle, then sew ½″ gold braid in a trellis design with 1″ space between each strip, securing all places where the braid meets by sewing on a large pearl bead. Fit this into the circle. Cut a piece of chiffon or voile into a semi-circular flare and attach to the back of the roll for about 6″, then cut a crossway piece, 18″ wide by 22″ long, pleat lengthwise into folds until about 3″ wide, attach to the roll at both sides to grip over the ears and under the chin.

A CROWN—This is a simple design but it can be varied and made to any design or size required. Make a paper pattern first Fold a piece of paper double, draw a slight semicircular line from centre front, dropping to 2″ at the side, to head size required, allowing 1″ at each side for overlapping. Design the spires or battlements, cut out and unfold. Then both sides are alike. Place patterns on buckram, cut out and overlap back seam, oversew wire on to all edges on wrong side. Sew $\frac{1}{4}$″ piping cord on all edges on right side, coat with gold metallic paint all over, allow to dry, then glue or sew $\frac{1}{2}$″ coloured jewels in places required.

Another method is to cut the crown in felt, glueing it on to gold metallic american cloth, overlap at back, sew gold metallic braid or cord to all edges, and place the jewels. Wired edges are not necessary in this instance. Gold and silver plastic american cloth can be obtained from theatrical material suppliers.

The use of millinery wire on edges of hats and head dresses is to help keep the shape. If it is not used these would soon collapse. When using wire on felt the correct way is to sew the wire $\frac{1}{4}$″ up from the edge on the wrong side, then turn the felt edge up over it. This is also the method on stiff muslin, fine buckram and sparterie, but on stiff furnishing buckram, it is oversewn on the wrong side and the edge bound. When making stand-up bows and loops of ribbon, attach a piece of wire in each loop, which will prevent flopping. In the twenties and thirties there were large hats of layers of tulle, which were placed over wire shapes, being large cartwheels of wire twisted and fixed by expert milliners, of the old school. It is only in workrooms where there are such artistes that these hats can now be made.

Ostrich plumes, feather trimmings, artificial flowers and fruit and ribbons by the yard, can be obtained from millinery suppliers.

142

There are also a variety of straw trimmings sold by the piece, which are mainly used for making hats, by joining together and shaping, but unless one is an expert it would be useless to try this. These trimmings are, however, very good for decorating hats. Two millinery suppliers are:—

Rubans de Paris,
39a Maddox Street,
London, W.1.

Paul Craig,
5 Noel Street,
London, W.1.

The theatrical material suppliers mentioned are:—

B. Burnet & Co., Ltd.,
22 Garrick Street,
London W.C.2.

Index

Index

148